STEP UP TO THE PLATE

Intercessory Prayer: A study guide

SANDI UNDERWOOD

Step Up To The Plate
Intercessory Prayer: A study guide
by Sandi Underwood

Printed in the United States of America

ISBN 978-1-60477-315-6

www.xulonpress.com

ENDORSEMENTS

"Prayer is proof of spiritual life. Intercessory prayer is to act between two parties to bring them together or to ask a superior for the need of another.. It is a selfless ministry for others. Sandi Underwood challenges and offers practical help for those who would dare to live as priests in the presence of God for others." **Dr. Les Frazier, Ph.D. International Representative for Baptist International Missions**

"*Intercessory Prayer: A Study Guide* presents a practical procedure for praying. The prayer tools found in each section of the book have proven effective for serious prayer warriors. This study guide is a must read for the dedicated student of prayer." **Carl J. Vonnoh, Jr., MRE, CLAIM Director for Baptist International Missions, Inc.**

DEDICATION

I want to dedicate this book to my daughter, Shannon. Thank you for being such an encouragement to me. Thank you for your love, support and those kind words, "Mom, I'll buy your book, at least you'll have one sale". Thank you for putting together the web site and all the other little things you've done to help me complete this project. I love you, Mom.

ACKNOWLEDGEMENTS

Thank you

To Charles and Amy Gregory for their knowledge and wisdom in editing this work for me and for their love, patience, prayer and enduring friendship.

To Helen Franklin who was my prayer partner throughout this study. Thank you for faithfully meeting with me every week for our prayer time. Without your prayers I would never have made it through to the end. Thank you for all of your encouragement.

To Jerry LaPee who followed God's command and with fear and trepidation came to my house to talk to me about the Lord. I was saved two days after her wedding anniversary (remember how sick you were) on July 18, 1978.

To Glenda Vonnoh, who has always been an encourager in anything I have ever endeavored to do, who has always seen me through the eyes of a person who sees no wrong. As many mistakes as I have made in the past 29 years I have known her, she has never pointed out a fault, and I have many. If ever a person could walk on water because of another person's outlook I would definitely be able to walk on water.

A special thanks to Debbi Sharon who has stood by me through some of the roughest times in the last several years. She was used of God to advance my spiritual growth while I was writing this study (although more often than not she was not aware of how God was using her during this time).

CONTENTS

Introduction xv

SECTION I: Shall We Pray 21

SECTION II: What is Intercessory Prayer? 33

SECTION III: Satanic Attacks 45

SECTION IV: Patience and Perseverance 55

SECTION V: Stand in the Gap 65

SECTION VI: Praying God's Will 77

SECTION VII: Confidence and passion in Prayer 95

SECTION VIII: Does Fasting have a Place?..107

SECTION IX: The Beginning...119

FORWARD

Dear Prayer Warrior,

I Know that above all else our relationship and fellowship with God is the most important addition we can make to our life, and I believe Prayer is one of the most important factors in that relationship. Thank you for joining me in the journey of prayer, thank you for wanting to "Step up to the Plate" and become an intercessory prayer warrior.

I have written this study with the busy person in mind. Between Church, job, family, teaching Sunday school and serving on committees it can feel like a tug-a-war. Sometimes I think if I add just one more event to my already busy schedule I will go insane. Surely I will lose my mind. So the thought of even one more thing to do is like saying "clean your room" to a teenager. Ugh, how can I find the time, yet over the last two years God has helped me rise early to pray, do research, read books on prayer, and write this study before going to work.

I have intentionally kept this book short and have tried to stay away lengthy prose. I tried to follow that old Dragnet saying (for those of you who remember Sgt. Joe Friday): "Just the facts, ma'am, just the facts!" I believe I have succeeded in making this study as I imagined: light, easy to read, practical, and a study that will not boggle the mind.

I pray that as you go through this you will learn the biblical meaning of Intercessory Prayer, see biblical examples and real life illustrations of answered prayer and that you will be encouraged to take your personal prayer life and your personal relationship with God to a higher level.

In Christian Love,

Sandi Underwood

INTRODUCTION

Proverbs 16:1 "The preparations of the heart in man, and the answer of the tongue, is from the LORD."

When God began to impress on me that I should write a study on intercessory prayer I met his call with doubt. My thought was, "You must be kidding". To which God replied, "No I'm not", and so it went back and forth until I finally accepted that it was God, not me, that came up with the idea. Then I headed for the prayer closet to ask God to guide and direct me in this endeavor and to dry up the ideas and words if it was not His leading.

I tried many times to escape the time and work involved in this project but never could get away from it. I asked God, Why? The Holy Spirit replied, "Because you are willing". "Yes, I answered, but not worthy. There are those much more qualified than I am." The Holy Spirit spoke again, "That may be so, but you are willing". As you can see, even after accepting the call, doubt still reared it ugly head. I knew I was willing, and I knew I loved to teach. This was a project, however, that I would not only be teaching, but I would be developing as well. I was apprehensive, still am, but I could not let go; the Holy Spirit would not allow me to let go. I knew God was commanding me to "step up to the plate", He was throwing the pitch and it was up to me to grab the bat and try to hit a home run.

There were so many others that were far wiser and more experienced than me, and that thought frightened me into a mass of research of already published works. My research included such authors as EM Bounds, Andrew Murray, Dutch Sheets, Cathy Jacobs, Jim Cymbala, Wycliff, Moody and many others. I think I gave new meaning to "surfing" the internet. I am grateful that so many have shared their experiences with the public and have given us the benefit of their experiences.

I have a habit of praying out loud so I am certain Satan heard all my plans and as a result I believe Satan knew my heart and was preparing for battle right from the start. I had various issues arise one after the other, back to back, that kept me in an emotional uproar. Family circumstances, personal battles, and personal relationships seemingly deteriorated before my eyes. I had allowed myself to become consumed and obsessed with the "Woe is me" times I was going through. I struggled for months, crying out to God, and yes, having an old-fashioned pity party. We've all been there. As I wept, struggled and wrestled, God told on me to "step through the barrier of pain and hurt and move on". God's Word tells us in:

Ephesians 6:12 "For we wrestle not against flesh and blood, but against principalities, against powers, against the rulers of the darkness of this world, against spiritual wickedness in high places."

I wrote out the words "step through the barrier of pain and hurt and move on" in my prayer book and repeated them over and over. Some may consider that "vain repetition" but it was not. It was a healthy reminder each day of the goal I was trying to reach. We must be careful not to confuse "vain repetitions" with continually talking to God about a problem that we have yet to resolve, or see resolved.

The details of these bombardments into, and on, my life are not as important as the fact they were happening. Without a doubt Satan would have loved nothing more than to have me step away from this work, because it would be easier to back off than to continue the fight. However, if we stop doing battle with Satan he will stop doing battle with us, when the battle is done Satan has won, and the work of God is left undone. If life is too easy, possibly, we are doing nothing of value for our Lord and Savior. I also prayed the "Warriors Prayer" daily from the Word of God.

Ephesians 6:13-17 "¹³⁾Wherefore take unto you the whole armour of God, that ye may be able to withstand in the evil day, and having done all, to stand.¹⁴⁾ Stand therefore, having your loins girt about with truth, and having on the breastplate of righteousness; ¹⁵⁾And your feet shod with the preparation of the gospel of peace; ¹⁶⁾Above all, taking the shield of faith, wherewith ye shall be able to quench all the fiery darts of the wicked. ¹⁷⁾And take the helmet of salvation, and the sword of the Spirit, which is the word of God:"

I began praying in earnest for relief and at the same time I dove headfirst into this study. Not too many days later I realized the experiences and the overwhelming bombardment, was necessary to further heighten my own understanding of what persistence in prayer and persistence in a relationship with Jesus was all about. It is about hard work and "glue" power. Sticking it out even when you are at a low point and it *appears* the hurt is just too difficult to overcome. It is all about keeping Satan from getting the victory. Far too often give up and we allow Satan to get the victory over our prayer life.

Our personal success as an Intercessor does not hinge on our personal emotions but on our personal relationship with God. If we can accept that most of our hurt and pain is because we set our expectations of a person or event higher than we set our expectations of God, then we can push through the barriers of pain and hurt. We can be *all that God wants us to be*, for His Glory and Honor through persistent and powerful prayer.

I praise God for standing by my side, through the best and worst of my battle with Satan. I assure you that God did not mind one bit that I kept repeating myself. The only ones that get upset when you repeat yourself are your kids and some of your friends. God is the greatest friend we can have. Unlike us, He is patient and kind. It does not bother Him in the least if it takes us more than one prayer time to find a resolution to our problem.

Why should we study about intercessory prayer? Why not just meet and pray about needs and any other concern that comes to mind? What is the difference between our daily prayers and an intercessory prayer? How can being an intercessor change the way we pray? Will it change what we pray about or whom we pray for?

As we go through this study my prayer is that we will find the answer to these questions and more. I pray that God will give us a deeper understanding of intercessory prayer and that we will develop a closer relationship with Him. I have intentionally kept each section short. I want us to grasp the meat of the subject and not become bogged down with too much academia. I want us to have time to stop and pray. But we must keep in mind Luther's Maxim: "To have prayed well is to have studied well." Get your texts, your thoughts, and your words from God.

Thank you for partnering with me in this study on intercessory prayer. As we go through this study I believe we will come to realize there is no greater need in our Church and our Nation today than people who will commit themselves to a prayer life led by the Holy Spirit. People who will pray needs assigned them by the Holy Spirit, persistently praying through until you God reveals to them that it is time to leave that prayer need and move on. We may not know how God is going to answer our prayer, but in our heart we just know He is, and He will handle it for His honor and His glory.

Describe your heart for prayer and why you believe this study will help you? _____

_____

_____

_____

_____

_____

SECTION I:

SHALL WE PRAY?

Matthew 18:19 "Again I say unto you, That if two of you shall agree on earth as touching any thing that they shall ask, it shall be done for them of my Father which is in heaven."

Why don't we begin by answering the question "Shall we pray"? With a hearty "yes"! Let's specifically pray that God will give us wisdom and understanding, that God will use us as Intercessory Prayer Warriors. Pray that God will direct our paths and lead us to succeed in our pursuit of an effective and rewarding prayer life.

🏛 Before we continue write a few sentences that describe what you believe it will take to become a successful Intercessory Prayer warrior? There is no right or wrong response.

_____

_____

_____

_____

_____

To be successful as Intercessory Prayer warriors we must allow our body to become a House of Prayer.

Matthew 21:13 "And said unto them, It is written, My house shall be called the house of prayer; but ye have made it a den of thieves."

I realize Jesus was talking about the Jerusalem Temple and the money changers but let's stretch it and consider our body as the house of prayer.

I Corinthians 6:19-20 "(19)What? know ye not that your body is the temple of the Holy Ghost which is in you, which ye have of God, and ye are not your own? (20)For ye are bought with a price: therefore glorify God in your body, and in your spirit, which are God's."

Is it such a big stretch to say that our body, our temple, which is called "*the house of God*", should also be called "*the house of Prayer*"?

We must free our body from sinful influences as much as is humanly possible, free from the influences of worldliness that clutter our mind with ungodly thoughts and our body with ungodly substances. We should be careful what we allow our eyes to see and what we allow ourselves to take in. I do not see a need to elaborate with a laundry list of sinful thoughts and actions. God can and will, if you ask, provide you with your personal list of what you need to get rid of. This thought leads us to the next step, which should be a willingness to clean house. ***Psalm 51:10 tells us: "Create in me a clean heart, O God; and renew a right spirit within me."***

If our hearts are not clean and purified before God he cannot hear our prayers. We cannot harbor ill towards another; bitterness, anger, hatred, unforgiveness, and the multitude of other sins that we sometimes hold deep within us. We must come before God repentant and willing to allow Him to purge us. We must try to wash off each item on our laundry list that God has said to get rid of. We must set aside anything that interferes with our relationship with God. **Hebrews 12:1 reads in part:** *"…..let us lay aside every weight, and the sin which doth so easily beset us, and let us run with patience the race that is set before us,"*

What do you believe might be preventing you from having a clean heart? What is that "weight" that is hindering your prayer life? _____

_____

_____

_____

_____

Notice the word "and" between "weight" and "sin". This implies that sometimes we allow worldly pursuits to interfere in our relationship with God. It might be something that, in and of itself, may not be a sin, such as an association with another person. Possibly you have placed your need for this person above your need for God. How about material wealth, pleasure, entertainment, or any myriad of things designed to titillate the human mind and body. Is there a person, a sport, a hobby or anything that you are placing above your need for God?

What is it that is holding you back? What area of your life do you need to give to God that will allow you to become a clean vessel? Are you ready to pour out your heart and soul? Are you ready for God to receive your heart and soul?

We need to let go of the *weight* or *sin* that is holding us in bondage and allow God to clean us, to scrub off all the filth, leaving us with an unselfish desire to commune and fellowship with God. We must allow the Holy Spirit to speak to us, lead us, and point our prayers in the direction God wishes us to go. We must pray for God's guidance and for the Holy Spirit to make our direction in prayer clear to us. Only then will the Holy Spirit tell us on whose behalf He wishes us to intercede. I hope as we go through this study you will experience the power of the Holy Spirit in your prayer life.

🏛 Go back to the list you made a few paragraphs ago. Can you add to it? Stop now and pray that God will help you with your list. Write down one item that stands out above the others that you believe is the major stumbling block in your prayer life. _____

_____

_____

_____

_____

Wouldn't it be wonderful to have an awareness of God's presence in the same way Abraham felt His presence? Let's look for a moment at Abraham's relationship with God.

Abraham was known as a ***Friend of God***. The following scriptures talk about their relationship.

> ***II Chronicles 20:7 "Art not thou our God, who didst drive out the inhabitants of this land before thy people Israel, and gavest it to the seed of Abraham thy friend for ever?"***
>
> ***Isaiah 41:8 "But thou, Israel, art my servant, Jacob whom I have chosen, the seed of Abraham my friend."***
>
> ***James 2:23 "And the scripture was fulfilled which saith, Abraham believed God, and it was imputed unto him for righteousness: and he was called the Friend of God."***

Dutch Sheets, in his book "The Beginners Guide to Intercession" put it this way; "He wasn't God's Friend because he was an *intercessor;* he was an *intercessor* because he was God's Friend".[1] We must, through our life, our actions, our relationships, but primarily through our prayer life, become "A Friend of God".

To become a friend of God requires obedience, another step in our preparation for a life of Intercessory prayer. There are times when not only is obedience to God's Word expected, but God will ask you to do something out of the ordinary. When I began this study I realized the Holy Spirit was working on me to give up my need to have my worth and character, my existence, validated by a particular person. Their approval was becoming more important than God's approval. I did not realize this until one morning in prayer God pointed out this stumbling block in my life. I was shocked, but on further reflection and prayer I knew it was true. We all have a desire to be seen as a worthwhile person. We have that human want to be needed and loved by others. Seek God's validation of your worth through the reading of His Word and through prayer. God will send human reinforcements to shore us up during those times when we are feeling worthless and unloved. The key is going to God first.

🏛 What is it that may be keeping you from a close, prayerful, relationship with God? __

_____

_____

_____

_____

God validates us, tests and proves us. God was asking me to set aside my need for human approval and release my heart to Him, accepting Him as the one who accepts me. Although human encouragement and support are good, I had to learn that it was only important that God, and God alone, approved of me. I had to set aside hurt feelings, a hurt caused by my expectations of another person. God was asking me to step aside in the relationship, a relationship I was smothering to death anyway. I had to clean up my act at the command of God to continue with this study.

One of the most remarkable stories of obedience involved me. Although I was not the one being obedient, it was others being obedient to God's call to witness to me. That may sound like a reasonably easy task on the surface but for Jerry it was a massive hurdle to overcome. I did not live far from Calvary Baptist Church and the church had a day care center. I chose the Calvary Day Care Center for my daughter. If I try to tell the entire testimony it would take several chapters so I will give one sentence that I believe will help explain the fear and trepidation with which Jerry and Kim had before coming to visit. One of the women at the day care center nicknamed me "wood the hood". Mind you I did not look at myself as a rough and tough person. I made certain I was sober and my cigarette was out before I went in. I checked all inappropriate language at the door. I was proud of those little acts of charity. I did not know that my demeanor was speaking louder than my charitable actions. I guess being six foot, having a deep voice and a sharp tongue might have had something to do with how I was perceived.

To move on with the story, Jerry and Kim got up the nerve one visitation night to come to my house. This was after the day care women had prayed for several years. It is difficult not to tell the whole story but my testimony is not the point as much as their obedience to God. They came to my house and again I was on what I thought was my best outward behavior. I knew when I sat Jerry in a chair with the collapsing legs (they didn't) and Kim placed her Bible in the middle of my coffee table that I was going to hear the God talk. I did. When they left I walked them to their car and Jerry had the boldness to say, "You know just enough Bible to hang yourself", I went back in the house and had a beer. Undoubtedly they went home to pray.

Their obedience to God in 1978 is why I know Christ as my Savior and why today I am writing this study on Intercessory Prayer. Were it not for Day Care full of praying women and two women's obedience to God's call to come knocking on my door I would be bound for

Hell, if not already dead and in Hell. Witnessing is tough enough, but how about believing you were going to witness to a "hood"? When I found out what they called me I wasn't so certain I shouldn't have been afraid of me.

🏛 When you read this story what was your first reaction? What would you have done?

_____

_____

_____

_____

🏛 Has God asked you to do something that was uncomfortable? If so, what was it? _____

_____

_____

_____

_____

Obedience entails our believing God's Word and living God's Word to the best of our ability. These are just a few of the scriptures that command obedience in our prayer life.

> *Matthew 26:41 "Watch and pray, that ye enter not into temptation: the spirit indeed is willing, but the flesh is weak."*
>
> *Colossians 4:2 "Continue in prayer, and watch in the same with thanksgiving;"*
>
> *I Thessalonians 5:17 "Pray without ceasing."*
>
> *Romans 12:12 "Rejoicing in hope; patient in tribulation; continuing instant in prayer;"*

Strong's Concordance[2] references pray, prayed, prayer, prayers, prayest, and praying close to one thousand times. Unless you think I took time to count every verse referenced I will confess that I measured how many lines were in an inch, measured the number of inches, and multiplied. The point is there are close to 1000 references so no matter how you do the calculations that places a high degree of importance on prayer.

Sadly, we do not practice intercessory prayer a great deal in our modern day churches. I suppose in our technologically savvy world we have become too intelligent, or perhaps just too busy, to be obedient to God. I suppose you could say we have placed our worldly needs above God's biblical command to pray, and in so doing we have lost the power of intercessory prayer.

Genesis 22: 17-18 "[17]That in blessing I will bless thee, and in multiplying I will multiply thy seed as the stars of the heaven, and as the sand which is upon the sea shore; and thy seed shall possess the gate of his enemies; [18]And in thy seed shall all the nations of the earth be blessed; because thou hast obeyed my voice."

I think what we have failed to realize is when God referred to Abraham's seed (his descendants), that WE are Abraham's seed. All of us, including Abraham, have our roots in Adam and Eve. It only follows genealogically that if we have our roots, our beginning, in Adam and Eve then we, Abraham and us, are descendants of Adam and Eve and so we are descendants of, or the seed of Abraham.

Matthew Henry[3] explains it this way: "The covenant was to be accomplished in due time. The promised Seed was Christ and Christians in him. And all who are of faith are blessed with faithful Abram, being partakers of the same covenant blessings. In token of this covenant his name was changed from Abram, 'a high father,' to Abraham, 'the father of a multitude.' All that the Christian world enjoys, they are indebted to Abraham and his Seed."

What effect do you think being a descendent of Abraham should have on our position as a Christian? _____

_____

_____

_____

_____

Many people believe Abraham was a Jew. He was neither Jew nor Arab but as the father of Ishmael and the great-grandfather of Judah he was an ancestor of both. Abraham was a Hebrew. At the time of Abraham's birth Israelites and Jews were not in existence. The children of Jacob were the first Israelites and through Isaac's son, Judah, we see the first Jews.

In reading through the genealogy in Matthew 1:1-17 you will notice that Christ is traced back to Abraham through his legal father Joseph. In verses 18-25 you will recognize that scripture proves Joseph was not Christ's physical father. This shows our link to the everlasting covenant given to Abraham by God and the covenant of everlasting life given to us by Christ's death on the cross. I call it the "tie that binds" us to Abraham and to our Lord and Savior, Jesus Christ. We are bound by being Children of God and by being descendants of Abraham (through Adam and Eve), to the covenants of Abraham and to the promises of God through Christ, promises we can call on through prayer. Understanding of course this does make us covenant Christian's, we are not under the law. We are Christians saved by grace through the blood of Christ, genealogically tied to Abraham.

How exciting it is to learn the promise in Genesis 22:17-18 also applies to us. We are of the seed of Abraham, the descendants of Abraham. With our heritage, our line straight back to the most faithful of Men of God, it should make us want to follow their lead and keep a close relationship with God our Father through prayer.

What excites you most about being a descendent of Abraham?_____

_____

_____

_____

_____

As we begin our walk toward an effective intercessory prayer life we should heed the following advice.

Psalms 27:14 "Wait on the LORD: be of good courage, and he shall strengthen thine heart: wait, I say, on the LORD."

As an impatient people we need to learn to "wait" if we are to be effective intercessors. So often we pray "once" about something and that's that. If we receive no immediate response we give up. Most of us are impatient and hate the "waiting game". Standing in line at the grocery store we tap our feet, look at magazines, internally huff and puff, hurry! Hurry! Hurry! Why is that cashier so slow? We tie ourselves up in knots. We wait, we pay and we go. Our groceries are our reward...and yet we are still so impatient. We are an instant gratification, fast-food generation. We want it all now!!!!

Look back at Psalms 27:14. We are doing more than waiting on a grocery clerk; we are waiting on the Lord. We do not have a visual of what the Lord is doing; we are not standing in line. God is omniscient, and He hears us when we speak. Our problem is we want the answer now. "OK God, I asked, so let me in on the secret, what's the answer"...and I want to know now! In the Army we had a saying that went "hurry up and wait". We are in such a hurry to get what we want or get where we want to go. I guess we could alter it a bit and have our own little saying, "hurry up (to pray) and wait (for the answer)". Waiting on God requires faith in

God's wisdom and God's timing. The best in life is worth waiting for and God is the best we have in this life.

Romans 8:27-28 "(27)And he that searcheth the hearts knoweth what is the mind of the Spirit, because he maketh intercession for the saints according to the will of God. (28)And we know that all things work together for good to them that love God, to them who are the called according to his purpose."

Whatever the answer, however long it takes to get the answer, we can take comfort in knowing the answer will work for the good of the one doing the praying and the one prayed for. We can take refuge in the knowledge that while we are interceding for others the Holy Spirit is interceding for us. Wow! What a great prayer chain: Us, the Holy Spirit, Jesus the Son and God the Father. It just doesn't get any better than that.

As we end this section write God a prayer asking Him to help you to be more courageous in your prayer life, ask Him to strengthen your heart. _____

_____

_____

_____

_____

Closing Moments:

1. My _____ shall be called a _____ of _____.

2. _____ in me a _____ heart, oh God.

3. What does Hebrews 12:1 tell us to do? _____

4. What step is required to become a friend of God? _____

5. What does Psalm 27:14 tell us to do? _____

6. What promise does Romans 8:27 give us? _____

_____

SECTION II:

<u>WHAT IS INTERCESSORY PRAYER</u>

Genesis 18:31-33 "*[31)]*And he said, Behold now, I have taken upon me to speak unto the LORD: Peradventure there shall be twenty found there. And he said, I will not destroy it for twenty's sake. *[32)]*And he said, Oh let not the LORD be angry, and I will speak yet but this once: Peradventure ten shall be found there. And he said, I will not destroy it for ten's sake. *[33)]*And the LORD went his way, as soon as he had left communing with Abraham: and Abraham returned unto his place.*"

What a powerful example of intercessory prayer, of letting God define what we should be doing. Abraham persevered and never gave up. Abraham pleaded his case and God agreed. God agreed because it is always God's will to see men and nations saved. Abraham was praying in God's will. Unfortunately if men and nations continue in their sinful ways God will destroy them, just as he did Sodom and Gomorrah.

Wycliffe's Bible Encyclopedia[4] defines intercession as "to appeal or petition" from the Greek word *entygchano*. Further it is defined as: "to fall in with a person, to draw close to him so as to enter into familiar speech and communion with him…implies, it is free familiar prayer, such as boldly draws near to God". Wycliffe continues to say that "intercession, then, highlights naturalness, boldness, and familiarity in prayer".

The Living Webster Encyclopedic Dictionary[5] gives this definition: "to intercede: To act between parties with a view to reconciling their differences or points of contention; mediate; to plead or interpose on behalf of another; Intercession: The act of interceding; mediation; entreaty, prayer, or petition in behalf of another."

   ⛪ In Genesis 18:31-33 quoted above what did Abraham say that supports Wycliff's definition of Intercession as "to draw close to him so as to enter into familiar speech and communion with him"? _____

_____

_____

_____

_____

I realize these definitions are lengthy but I believe if we are to become fully involved in intercessory prayer we should have a biblically sound understanding of just what intercessory prayer is.

II Corinthians 5:18-19 "[18)]And all things are of God, who hath reconciled us to himself by Jesus Christ, and hath given to us the ministry of reconciliation; [19)]To wit, that God was in Christ, reconciling the world unto himself, not imputing their trespasses unto them; and hath committed unto us the word of reconciliation."

Ezekiel 22:30 "And I sought for a man among them, that should make up the hedge, and stand in the gap before me for the land, that I should not destroy it: but I found none."

It is my understanding that we are responsible to God to act as intercessors for the Children of God, going before God with all the strength and power we can muster, pleading with God on their behalf. Do we pray as intercessors on behalf of another? Do we plead with God to intercede on their behalf?

I believe our normal way of working is to approach God with some words of praise, a personal need and then move on to the needs of someone else, briefly offering up a need on their behalf. We might stick with it for five or ten minutes, sometimes we may even get in a full thirty minutes. While we are at it we may try to parade another dozen people from our "Hit Parade of Prayer" list we picked up at church. You might ask, what's wrong with that? Isn't the whole idea of intercessory prayer, to pray for others, of course the answer is yes, and no?

🏛 Take a moment and jot down how you view yourself as an intercessory prayer warrior?

_____

_____

_____

_____

_____

To be a powerful intercessor you must be in _agreement_ with, and in _fellowship_ with, God.

I Corinthians 1:9-10 "9)God is faithful, by whom ye were called unto the fellowship of his Son Jesus Christ our Lord. 10)Now I beseech you, brethren, by the name of our Lord Jesus Christ, that ye all speak the same thing, and that there be no divisions among you; but that ye be perfectly joined together in the same mind and in the same judgment."

James 5:16-18 "[16]Confess your faults one to another, and pray one for another, that ye may be healed. The effectual fervent prayer of a righteous man availeth much. [17]Elias was a man subject to like passions as we are, and he prayed earnestly that it might not rain: and it rained not on the earth by the space of three years and six months. [18]And he prayed again, and the heaven gave rain, and the earth brought forth her fruit."

When we pray for our friend or neighbor we are praying exactly what they asked us to pray; not necessarily praying in agreement with God. We may also be praying for ten people when God wants us to take a break and pray for one particular need. Confusing? Simply put, when we decide to intercede on someone's behalf we must first ask the Holy Spirit to help us, to guide us and lead us in the direction God wants us to pray. Then our prayer can be "the effective, fervent prayer of a righteous man".

In a book entitled <u>Rees Howells, Intercessor</u> author Norman Grubb[6] brought out three things to be seen in an intercessor that are not normally found in ordinary prayer:

(1) **Identification**: Identifying with the one for whom you intercede and as far as possible taking their place.

(2) **Agony**: Self must be released from itself to become the agent of the Holy Ghost. Scripture says the Holy Spirit makes intercession for us.

Romans 8:26 "Likewise the Spirit also helpeth our infirmities: for we know not what we should pray for as we ought: but the Spirit itself maketh intercession for us with groanings which cannot be uttered."

(3) **Authority**: Intercession so identifies the intercessor with the sufferer that it gives him a prevailing place with God. He moves God. Mr. Howell's referred to George Muller's experience. Mr. Mueller's place of intercession was for the orphans. Mr. Mueller was always ready to be the first sufferer in their behalf.

🏛 Can you think of someone you identify with in their need? Place their name here, stop and pray for them now? _____

_____

_____

_____

_____

Grubb[7] also made this statement: "A prayer warrior can pray for a thing to be done without necessarily being willing for the answer to come through himself; and he is not even bound to continue in the prayer until it is answered. But an intercessor is responsible to gain his objective, and he can never be free until he has gained it. He will go to any lengths for the prayer to be answered through Him."

That is a powerful statement and a difficult position to take. That is one man's outlook on what an intercessor is to be. Maybe you are already there, as Rees Howells was, or perhaps you are between the everyday pursuit of prayer and the complete giving over of your physical, mental and emotional being to finding an answer through intercessory prayer. I don't believe there is a hard-and-fast definition for the difference, but I do believe you will find the answer as you become more and more deeply involved in your prayer life for others.

This places a heavy responsibility on those of us who decide to become intercessory prayer partners with God. God wants to use you and me on this earth; He wants to work through us to carry out His will. Can God use us to carry out His will? Or are we just bystanders occupying the earth until the Lord returns?

How does this work? Let's take a look. You may be praying down your "list" when suddenly God impresses on your heart to pray for one specific person. You sense a burden that weighs heavy on your heart, a deep need to cry out to God for just that particular need. Maybe God has asked you to pray for someone that needs healing from a devastating illness or disease.

Are you willing to allow God to use you to answer the need of the person you prayed for above? Are you willing to continue in prayer for them until God meets their need? What is God's direction for you? _____

_____

_____

_____

_____

People have many different needs. We are going to consider healing in this scenario, because it seems to be the most prevalent and stressful need in people's lives today. After many hours, days or months of prayer God may give you the peace and knowledge that healing is going to take place. It is also possible God may direct you to pray for comfort and strength for the family. God may be revealing to you the person you are praying for is not going to be healed. (A word of caution is in order. When this happens PLEASE DO NOT tell the family that you've had a revelation from God and their loved one is going to die.) Keep it between you and God, recognizing that God is in control. God does not expect, nor want, us to go around bragging, bringing attention to ourselves.

Your prayer just might be the prayer that makes the difference between a positive or a negative answer. That's why you must always go into prayer believing God for a miracle and let God lead you. God's miracle may not be what we imagine; it may not be the miracle we conjure up in our mind. Therefore our faith must be strong. We must believe that God will hear our prayer that God will talk to us, lead us, guide us and direct us in our prayer life. We must also recognize that when we enter into intercessory prayer there is no guarantee that God is going to reveal His plan to us. Sometimes God just wants us to pray in a certain direction and wait with everyone else to see the results.

God will tell you whether you need to keep praying or not, just not always why you need to keep praying. Currently I am continuing a prayer I have been praying for over a year. God has not released me from the prayer, or the direction of the prayer, at the same time others believe a positive answer is hopeless. Why isn't God releasing me from this prayer? Truthfully, I have no idea. I just cannot shake the belief that there is still hope. In God's time He will either show me the answer or release me from the burden.

Is there something you are praying about now that you believe God has kept on your heart, a burden he will not release you from? Write that burden here. How long have you carried this burden? _____

_____

_____

_____

_____

Romans 15:1-2 "[1]We then that are strong ought to bear the infirmities of the weak, and not to please ourselves. [2]Let every one of us please his neighbour for his good to edification."

We need to be careful that we don't become too impressed with ourselves and our abilities. As humans' humility does not come natural for us, as a consequence we allow ourselves to puff up when God reveals something to us. "Oh, aren't we just too special," and we want the world to know. This gives new meaning to "silence is golden". When we are in total agreement with God there will be times when we are agreeing to keep our mouth shut. I realize there are times when we do need to reveal what God has laid on our heart. Remember the portion of my testimony in Section I where the women came to my house. That was a time when they had to reveal what God had laid on their hearts. Their silence may well have been the end of me, or God just might have sent someone else. In this case silence would have meant one of us would be the loser.

I do not know of any instances where God has revealed a death to someone and then asked that person to tell the loved one. God has revealed to me on several occasions the person I am praying for will not be healed and He has done this well ahead of the time others were ready to admit medicine had done all it could. (Much more often he has withheld that information from me). Never did God ever ask me to tell the family, or friends, that their loved one was going to die. I did make the mistake several years ago of mentioning to one of my friends that a certain individual we were both praying for was not going to get better. In response she said, "You can't know that. You don't know what God is going to do. God can heal them". God can and often does, Praise the Lord, heal in a miraculous way. There have been many people that looked like they were at death's door that God has healed. On other occasions God has chosen to take the person home. If it is God's wish for you to know, you will know the outcome, good or bad. Does God always reveal the outcome in such a manner? Absolutely not! Oh, what big-headed, self-sufficient, self-righteous people we would become if that happened.

🏛 Can you recall a time when God revealed to you what the outcome would be and changed you direction in prayer? _____

_____

_____

_____

_____

I Timothy 2:5 "For there is one God, and one mediator between God and men, the man Christ Jesus; Hebrews 10:19 "Having therefore, brethren, boldness to enter into the holiest by the blood of Jesus,

Praying in agreement with, and in concert with, God's wishes and desires is not always popular and not always understood. Hopefully, over time, people will begin to recognize that you receive many answers to your prayers and will come to you with their needs. You do not need to search for people to pray for. God will send them to you, or God may simply lay someone on your heart and you might not have a clue what their need might be. Just pray.

Those that do not believe in such deep intercessory prayer will more than likely put you on their list of kooks to avoid. Consider this as no great loss because what you want is a life of prayer that not only reflects your agreement with God, but that brings you prayer partners of like mind who are in agreement with God as well.

It would be wise to keep in mind that not everyone is called to the same types of intercessory prayer. While some may believe they are called to intercede in the area of healing, others may believe they are called to intercede in the area of financial needs and others may believe they are called to intercede in the area of family needs. Some may believe they are "on call" intercessors. God calls on them and the nature of the need is inconsequential.

There are many other areas of need for intercessory prayer, such as the nation, the media, missionaries, teachers, and the list goes on. Remember, I mentioned earlier that intercessory prayer does not take the place of your everyday prayer life, that life of prayer where you offer up other's needs, as well as your own needs, daily.

The difference is the deep, burning, passionate desire for a particular situation, a particular need that God has placed on your heart to pray for deeply and without ceasing. Praying until God Himself reveals to you the answer or reveals that He has handled the matter, to what end you may never know.

Before moving on to the next section ask God to give you a special burden that is unique and separate from your regular prayer time. Record that burden here. _____

_____

_____

_____

_____

_____

Closing Moments

1. Wycliff says that intercession means to _____ or _____.

2. In II Corinthians 5:18 God has given us the ministry of _____.

3. To be a powerful intercessor you must be in _____ with and in _____ with God.

4. According to Norman Grubb, in his book <u>Rees Howells, Intercessor</u>[8] what three things can normally be seen in an intercessor? _____, _____, _____.

5. In Hebrews 10:19 we are told to have _____ to enter the _____ by the _____ of _____.

6. Name some of the areas of intercessory prayer we can become involved in._____

    _____

    _____

SECTION III.

SATANIC ATTACKS

"And though this world with devils filled should threaten to undo us, / We will not fear for God has willed his truth to triumph through us." —Martin Luther[9]

What a powerful statement. With good intentions we set out to pursue great works for God and without fail we will find Satan nipping at our heels. I mentioned in the introduction how Satan made a beeline for me the minute I agreed with God to do this study. I thought I had managed to work my way through the original bombardment of Satanic attacks but, lo and behold, just as I was ending Section II a new round of attacks reared their ugly head.

Although it might have been better to place this in the introduction I placed it in this section to stress that these attacks are continual. It does not matter where we are spiritually, or how much time we spend in prayer, Satan is unrelenting in his attacks on the praying and working Christian.

Satan not only came up with new stuff to torture me with but also brought back the old and rehashed it, testing me to see if the combination would do the trick. I know he believed if he doubled up he could get me to quit. There were several times when it was tempting to pack it in.

As I write this I am depressed and upset, lonely and friendless. I am grieved inside over all that is going on without. My heart is pierced and bleeding. I can imagine a bunch of little spear toting devils dancing around, poking their spears at me, provoking the depression and the hurt, all the while laughing at me. At the same time, as I continue writing and praying, I can picture them slowly scattering, darting back and forth trying to win the battle. I am writing and praying within the power and strength of God, without whom I could not carry on.

Has Satan begun his attack on you? How is this affecting you relationship with God?

_____

_____

_____

_____

_____

It is God, and God alone, who wields our sword and shield, fights our battles, and staves off Satan's evil advances as long as we, no matter how hard the task, continue in His service, doing His will, as He directs. I sincerely doubt this will be my last bout, my last attack, because I do not intend to walk away from God or the work He has given me to do. When Satan quits attacking that is when I need to start worrying. It can only mean I have stopped serving and let my heart grow cold.

I become discouraged during these battles but I take comfort in knowing that one of the greatest evangelists of all times suffered severe depression brought on by Satan's attacks. That great man was none other than Charles Haddon Spurgeon, and I quote:

"It is no secret the Prince of Preachers, Charles Haddon Spurgeon, suffered black periods of anguishing depression. His congregation at the Metropolitan Tabernacle was once amazed to hear Spurgeon begin a sermon from Isaiah 41:14 with these words in his introduction: *"I have to speak today to me, and whilst I shall be endeavoring to encourage those who are distressed and downhearted, I shall be preaching, I trust to myself, for I need something which shall cheer my heart — why I cannot tell, wherefore I do not know, but I have a thorn in the flesh, a messenger of Satan to buffet me; my soul is cast down within me; I feel as if I had rather die than live; all that God hath done by me seems to be forgotten, and my spirit flags and my courage breaks down … I need your prayers."* [10]

It is important that we shake off Satan and his attacks and refuse to allow him a foothold into our lives, our hearts and our minds. The flesh wants to give in to Satan's demands, wants to roll over and play dead. The flesh wants someone else to fight the battle. We crave peace and quiet. Satan feeds on these cravings, hoping to get the victory by letting even the smallest remnant of his spear remain stuck in our flesh. If we allow this the wound will fester and become a garbage can for Satan's refuse. We must be careful to take out every last scrap of the garbage infesting our lives so Satan has nothing to mix his rotting garbage with.

As I continue I am aware of the battle raging in my flesh. The flesh wants to give in but the Spirit wants me to keep marching forward. We must remember whom it is we are fighting, who we are wrestling with:

Ephesians 6:12 "For we wrestle not against flesh and blood, but against principalities, against powers, against the rulers of the darkness of this world, against spiritual wickedness in high places."

🏛 Let's write a prayer of victory over Satan and remember to refer to it throughout this study? _____

_____

_____

_____

This battle we are talking about is raging in me as I continue to write, but as I began this chapter the battle got worse, the attacks grew stronger. My prayer life took a nosedive into oblivion. Satan wanted me to float along in depression and unhappiness; his attacks were relentless, ensuring that my life was full of trials and tribulations.

As I mentioned previously, I knew Satan was poking into every area of my life: family, friends, work, Church. Satan has put his spear of doubt, his spear of depression, his spear of loneliness, his spear of unhappiness, to name just a few, into my flesh. Satan has struck every weakness I have and I have at the worst times felt such deep pain and hurt that I would stop the presses and give it a rest. The heart can only take so much before it needs to stop and heal itself. Satan, our adversary, a lying spirit, is always there to try to discourage us from God's work, from a life of prayer.

I Peter 5:8 "Be sober, be vigilant; because your adversary the devil, as a roaring lion, walketh about, seeking whom he may devour:"

Satan hovers over us encouraging us to walk away, promising us that if we will just back off, even just a little, everything will be better. Try it and guess what? Satan will give you peace; he will stop torturing you just to try to prove that he, Satan, is right. He whispers gently that it is better to take the easy way, the less painful path throughout this life, besides, who's to know? At this point know one knows I am writing this, therefore, Satan says, if no one knows you are doing this then no one will think the less of you for not doing this. How confusing is that? I guess it would make sense if you ignored reality: God knows.

Ultimately, in the end, when we hear the trumpet sound, the one we will answer too is God. This test is to prove who is more important, God or Satan? If we choose Satan then we will become a self-centered, selfish people, dried up and spiritless. If we choose God then we can rest in the confidence that, no matter the battle, God's Word will hold true and we will win, but it will be a hard fight. We must remember these words of God:

II Chronicles 20:15 "And he said, Hearken ye, all Judah, and ye inhabitants of Jerusalem, and thou king Jehoshaphat, Thus saith the LORD unto you, Be not afraid nor dismayed by reason of this great multitude; for the battle is not yours, but God's."

What is the main focus of attention by Satan in your life at this time?_____

_____

Are you letting God fight the battle for you?_____

_____

If not, stop now and ask God to be your warrior, your shield and defender.

As the battle rages on and we wade through the events of our daily life we can become so discouraged and downhearted. I think that is when we become like King David and plead with God, asking Him when the battle will be over, when will we sense God's presence around us and recognize his presence in our prayers.

During these times of despair we must make a choice, either let Satan win or turn to God. The choice should be obvious: we must turn to God if we are weak in our prayer life. What better way to shore ourselves up than to go to the Word of God. Let him speak to us through His Word until we are strong enough to speak to Him through our prayers.

Psalm 23 "1)How long wilt thou forget me, O LORD? for ever? how long wilt thou hide thy face from me? 2)How long shall I take counsel in my soul, having sorrow in my heart daily? how long shall mine enemy be exalted over me? 3)Consider and hear

me, O LORD my God: lighten mine eyes, lest I sleep the sleep of death; ⁴⁾Lest mine enemy say, I have prevailed against him; and those that trouble me rejoice when I am moved. ⁵⁾But I have trusted in thy mercy; my heart shall rejoice in thy salvation. ⁶⁾I will sing unto the LORD, because he hath dealt bountifully with me."

I find it encouraging to realize that David, described as a man after Gods own heart, a mighty warrior of God, felt the same way I do, fought the same battles I fight, but went on to serve God triumphantly. Throughout all the trials and tribulations, even when David fell into temptation and sinned with exuberance, he still sought the face and forgiveness of God and continued to serve God.

I am not suggesting we give in to temptations and then hope to justify our sins by doing God's work. Without repentance our work would be worthless. What I am saying is that if you have fallen under the spell of Satanic attacks go to God and seek his forgiveness, repent, and keep on keeping on for God. It is the only way to defeat Satan.

Not all attacks will be of the same intensity for everyone, but you can rest assured that Satan has a plan for you if he thinks your intent is to follow God's plan for your life. When you have carried out one job for God and you undertake another, buck up, you are in for another of Satan's attacks. You will come under attack as you do this study and begin to engage in some intense prayer. The last thing in the world Satan wants is for Christians to pray. Satan will do everything in his power to pull you away from a life of prayer, to pull you away from God. Prayer is our best defense against Satan.

It would be remiss on my part to only mention the attacks by Satan and the certainty of their happening without mentioning the certainty of victory. God's word is balanced, not only revealing the truth about Satan and his dislike for Christians, but also revealing the solutions to Satan's dislike and personal attacks on us.

A lack of forgiveness is one of the most prevalent areas in our lives that Satan uses to hamper us in our prayer life.

II Corinthians 2:10-11 *"(10)To whom ye forgive any thing, I forgive also: for if I forgave any thing, to whom I forgave it, for your sakes forgave I it in the person of Christ; (11)Lest Satan should get an advantage of us: for we are not ignorant of his devices."*

I can only infer from this scripture that if we have an unforgiving heart then we are doomed in our battle to dislodge Satan's impact on our prayer life, as well as our everyday life. We must be careful to search our hearts for even the smallest morsel of unforgiveness that we might be chewing on.

We often overlook the little annoyances and concentrate on the large and obvious things that affect our relationship with God. Usually, it is the little annoyances that we fail to forgive which cause the greatest gap in our relationship with God. We quickly recognize and forgive the obvious, for example if a person were to slap you, you might turn the other cheek, be generous is your forgiveness of that individual. You may even forgive a thief using the tried and true, "well they must have needed it more than me". But what about that person you think lied about you, or revealed a secret you shared with them? How about the person who spread a tidbit of gossip that made you look bad? Emotional wounds are harder to forgive than physical wounds because our minds do not want to let go of hurt or wounded pride, forgiveness becomes a battle of the wits.

🏛 Why not go to the Lord in prayer right now and ask God to reveal any kernel of unforgiveness you might be harboring. Write down whatever it is and continue to pray until you are released from that burden of unforgiveness. _____

It's like being able to see the large rock in the road that we need step around so we can continue our travels, but we miss the small pebbles. Pebbles that can be such an annoyance as they constantly push up on the bottom of the foot, until the pain gets so great we finally give up. It's the little things, those small annoyances that we fail to forgive, that cause us the greatest grief and hindrance in our Christian prayer life. We need to rake up the pebbles of unforgiveness, ridding ourselves of those hindrances that give Satan the upper hand in our lives.

Romans 16:19-20 "[19]For your obedience is come abroad unto all men. I am glad therefore on your behalf: but yet I would have you wise unto that which is good, and simple concerning evil. [20]And the God of peace shall bruise Satan under your feet shortly. The grace of our Lord Jesus Christ be with you. Amen."

God will crush Satan on our behalf. Obedience to God insures victory over Satan. Our universal obedience list is the Ten Commandments, but it is the individual areas of obedience that are different for each individual that we cannot address here because God asks different things of each of us. When I talk of obedience in this manner I am not talking about sinful behavior, I am talking about obedience in service to God.

God may ask one to teach, another to preach, another to work in the nursery and another to do heaven only knows. The point is that whatever God asks us to do we must obey if we are to see the work of Satan crushed in our lives. Sounds simple but it is anything but simple. Anytime you go to battle it is tough and you can be sure Satan will see to that.

🏛 Is there something that God has asked you to do but you have yet to respond to God's call in the matter? _____

_____

_____

_____

_____

I want to close this section with a quote from Paul

I Corinthians 16:8-10 "(8)But I will tarry at Ephesus until Pentecost. (9)For a great door and effectual is opened unto me, and there are many adversaries. (10)Now if Timotheus come, see that he may be with you without fear: for he worketh the work of the Lord, as I also do."

Paul recognized that we have an adversary in Satan and that he uses people to carry out his task. It is no different today. Satan is the adversary and he uses the people around us to attack, to keep us off balance, with the hope that he will get the victory. To God be the glory, victory belongs to us through God.

🏛 Select a scripture that is personal to you. One you can recall during those times when you are under satanic attack. Commit the scripture to memory and use it freely when Satan comes to call. Write it here. _____

_____

_____

_____

_____

Closing Moments

1. Our greatest adversary in prayer is? _____

2. What does Ephesians 6:12 say about who we battle? _____

    _____

    _____

3. What are some of the spears that Satan throws at us? Can you think of some that were not

    mentioned? _____

    _____

4. I Peter 5:8 admonishes you to be _____ and be _____

5. II Chronicles 20:15 reminds us that the battle is _____

6. What is one of the most prevalent areas in our life that Satan uses to hamper our prayer time?

    _____

SECTION IV:

PATIENCE AND PERSERVANCE

I Peter 4:7 "But the end of all things is at hand: be ye therefore sober, and watch unto prayer."

We have all heard the comment "don't pray for patience, you just might be given something that requires it". We have already been given something that requires a great deal of patience and that something is prayer. How often have we started to pray and lost patience with the time and energy it takes. We let our minds wander off to some task we need to complete, we let our mind drift and mull over the days activities, or......... and the reasons go on. We may not label it at the time as losing patience, but it is, and with loss of patience comes loss of perseverance.

The dictionary definition of patience (patient) is:

"**Patience:** The act of being patient. Patient: Bearing pain or trial without complaining; sustaining afflictions with fortitude, calmness, or submission; long-suffering; persevering; able to bear."[11]

Notice the word "persevering" is in the definition of patient. How appropriate that the word persevere follows patience in the dictionary.

"Persevere: To continue resolutely in any enterprise undertaken, despite difficulties encountered; to pursue steadily any design or course begun."[12]

Without patience there is no perseverance, without perseverance we cannot expect answers to our prayers.

Prayer is hard work. It requires energy. It also requires you to have the "I'm going to stick-to-it" attitude. Like an old dog with a bone, you can't get the bone away from him until he is ready to let go. He cherishes that bone and will go so far as to hide it from us would be human thieves. Our prayers should be like that old bone. We hang on to our prayers until God tells us to let go, hiding them from our enemy, that old thief Satan, hiding them within the depths of our heart, pushing though for the Glory of God.

What "old bone" prayer are you praying? _____
Do you find it requires more energy than your regular prayer life? If so why do you
think that is the case? _____

_____

_____

Galatians 6:9 "And let us not be weary in well doing: for in due season we shall reap, if we faint not."

James 1:2-4 "2)My brethren, count it all joy when ye fall into divers temptations; 3)Knowing this, that the trying of your faith worketh patience. 4)But let patience have her perfect work, that ye may be perfect and entire, wanting nothing."

Prayer is an energetic endeavor that does not play well with a person who would be content to just lay back and play the role of a "couch potato". In Romans 15:30 Paul calls prayer a striving, he says *"Now I beseech you, brethren, for the Lord Jesus Christ's sake, and for the love of the Spirit, that ye strive together with me in your prayers to God for me;"*

Jacob wrestled, the Syrophenician woman struggled. Can we expect less of a battle? To have an effective and rewarding prayer life you must expend energy and approach your prayer closet with an attitude of patience and perseverance.

It is not enough to go on and on about how we should pray, how we should stick to it, how we should have patience, or how we should persevere. We need to see examples from God's Word to encourage us and lift us up. The following scriptures are just such examples:

Genesis 20:17-18 "(17)So Abraham prayed unto God: and God healed Abimelech, and his wife, and his maidservants; and they bare children. (18)For the LORD had fast closed up all the wombs of the house of Abimelech, because of Sarah Abraham's wife."

Deuteronomy 9:18-20 "(18) And I fell down before the LORD, as at the first, forty days and forty nights: I did neither eat bread, nor drink water, because of all your sins which ye sinned, in doing wickedly in the sight of the LORD, to provoke him to anger. (19)For I was afraid of the anger and hot displeasure, wherewith the LORD was wroth against you to destroy you. But the LORD hearkened unto me at that time also. (20)And the LORD was very angry with Aaron to have destroyed him: and I prayed for Aaron also the same time."

Isaiah 38:1-5 "(1)In those days was Hezekiah sick unto death. And Isaiah the prophet the son of Amoz came unto him, and said unto him, Thus saith the LORD, Set thine house in order: for thou shalt die, and not live. 2)Then Hezekiah turned his face toward the wall, and prayed unto the LORD, 3)And said, Remember now,

O LORD, I beseech thee, how I have walked before thee in truth and with a perfect heart, and have done that which is good in thy sight. And Hezekiah wept sore. 4)Then came the word of the LORD to Isaiah, saying, 5)Go, and say to Hezekiah, Thus saith the LORD, the God of David thy father, I have heard thy prayer, I have seen thy tears: behold, I will add unto thy days fifteen years."

Ephesians 6:18 "Praying always with all prayer and supplication in the Spirit, and watching thereunto with all perseverance and supplication for all saints;"

🏛 In what ways can you relate to these biblical men of prayer? Remember, there is no right or wrong response. _____

_____

_____

_____

_____

The greatest encouragement we can find to uplift our prayer life is in the Word of God. It is difficult for a Christian to continue praying for a specific concern when they do not see an immediate answer. You can see from the scriptures above that patience and perseverance was a necessity in the prayer lives of all great men of God. Despite hardships and difficulties they prayed for God to intervene, and God did intervene in many instances because of a prayer that would not cease.

We may lose patience when the effort becomes too painful or burdensome. Do you remember our definition of patient? In part it said "bearing pain or trial, sustaining affliction with fortitude, persevering".[13]

Romans 15:1-3 "1) We then that are strong ought to bear the infirmities of the weak, and not to please ourselves. 2)Let every one of us please his neighbour for his good to edification. 3)For even Christ pleased not himself; but, as it is written, The reproaches of them that reproached thee fell on me."

This can be spiritually, emotionally and physically exhausting and painful. In the verse above we can see that whatever the effort, we are to continue praying for others without thought of ourselves; to lift others and to glorify God through our prayers. God will be there for us, handling the struggle and bearing the reproach on our behalf, with a gentle hand, a strong arm and a compassionate heart attending to our every hurt and need. We can do no less for the ones we pray for.

🏛 Is there someone, or something, you can, and should be praying for that requires strength and energy on your part; a prayer that can turn into one of those all morning, exhausting, spiritually draining prayers? _____

🏛 Make a note of it here. _____

_____

_____

_____

_____

Colossians 4:12-13 "12)Epaphras, who is one of you, a servant of Christ, saluteth you, always labouring fervently for you in prayers, that ye may stand perfect and complete in all the will of God. 13)For I bear him record, that he hath a great zeal for you, and them that are in Laodicea, and them in Hierapolis."

Prayer is a time consuming commodity that is part of our spiritual life and spiritual growth. Prayer is our method of staying close to God and God staying close to us. Prayer is fellowship with God. Satan would like nothing better than to see our prayer life falter. Satan would like nothing better than to have Christians dry up and blow away. When we lose patience with our prayer life that is exactly what we do, we dry up and blow away spiritually.

Our inclination is to become impatient when we do not see immediate answers to our prayers. We give up on a subject before we have prayed it through because our nature is to move quickly from one task to another. Our attitude is: I have prayed, you answer, let's move on to the next problem. Now! This attitude runs parallel with our "McDonalds" life style: I have ordered, you serve, let's move on. Now!

We do not take time to savor the food (presence of God), enjoy (fellowship with God) and digest the food (wait on God for the answer). We quickly gobble down our food (call out our prayer) and move on (to the next task of the day).

The Word of God explains it this way:

Luke 11:9 "And I say unto you, Ask, and it shall be given you; seek, and ye shall find; knock, and it shall be opened unto you."

In short we are to patiently and with perseverance "keep on keeping on".

God can, and often does, choose to answer our prayers immediately. He just as easily may delay the answer because He has something better for us, if we patiently wait on Him. There are times when we are tired and worn out from praying for the same petition over and again and Satan steps in to "encourage" us to give up. Satan's big lie is that God doesn't care about the situation or He would have already done something about it. Don't let Satan fool you. God cares now and God has always cared about our needs, our petitions, and our prayers.

🏛 Can you remember a time when Satan "encouraged" you to give up on a particular prayer? Write the subject of the prayer here and briefly tell what happened.

_____

_____

🏛 What would you do differently now if you were in that same situation? _____

_____

_____

_____

Be faithful to your prayer life. Just as a cup fills up, one drop of water at a time, let your prayer cup fill up, one prayer at a time. When your prayers reach the top and are ready to spill over God reaches down and becomes the saucer that catches the spills, cleans up the mess, and answers your requests then and there. If the answers to our prayers come at a "snap of the finger", so to speak, we would become boastful and proud of our accomplishments. As prayer warriors we should be praising God for His accomplishments in answering our prayers. Remember, God is faithful and will always answer in His wisdom and in His timing.

Luke 18:1-8 tells the story of the widow woman who would not give up on her request for protection from the keeper of the gate. She did what some would call pestering, but what Jesus called persevering. She persisted in her pleas for protection until the keeper of the gate gave in and saw to her needs. Jesus' point was that if a judge or a keeper of the gate, who had no respect for God or people, would listen to someone who persevered, then God, who loves and cares for us, will be moved by our perseverance and patience.

🏛 Remember a time when God was faithful and wise in answering your prayer. I am sure you have multiple answers, but record the one that jumped out at you immediately?

_____

_____

_____

_____

_____

It is always encouraging to remember these times. Psalm 27:13 tells us that we can lose heart if we do not see the goodness of God. Turn now to Psalm 27:12-14 and read about God's strength and encouragement for us.

Luke 18:6-7: "6)And the Lord said, Hear what the unjust judge saith. 7)And shall not God avenge his own elect, which cry day and night unto him, though he bear long with them?"

We need to guard against giving up because things seem to be getting worse instead of better. Things may get worse, and often do, before they get better. The temptation is to doubt God's Word, doubt that God is going to answer our prayers. That can become fertile ground for Satan to take charge if we let him. We must go back to scripture when doubts attack us and stand fast in our determination to continue in prayer, without ceasing, without giving up.

The Bible gives us many examples of prayers and many examples of men and women of prayer, people who knew and recognized that God, and God alone, was the final authority in all we ask and for all our needs. In his book <u>Breakthrough Prayer</u> Jim Cymbala makes the statement "Prayer is heard and answered through "house rules" not our rules. We must ask according to God's Will, not our will."[14] If we keep that in mind it will do wonders for our ability to continue forward in our prayers and not give up.

We do not decide how we are to pray, that is God's decision. He makes the rules. His Word is our guide. We want quick answers to everything and we want to manipulate God into doing things our way. That is not prayer, prayer is a disciplined act based on obedience to the commands of God, followed through with persistence and consistence.

Patience and perseverance are keywords to a successful prayer life. Unfortunately too many of us have only one, or possibly neither, of these qualities. It takes a concerted effort on our part, a desire to touch God, to become closer to God and to overcome our natural state of impatience.

🏛 Imagine your prayer closet as having a front and a back door. Think about the last time you entered. Was it "in one door, out the other" or did you stop awhile and fill the closet with your prayers before you walked out? _____

_____

_____

_____

_____

Closing Moments

1. In what way should our prayer life be like an old dog with a bone? _____

   _____

2. What does Galatians 6:9 relay to us? _____

   _____

3. Jacob wrestling and the struggles of the Syrophenician woman remind us that prayer

   requires _____

4. Think of ways your prayer life resembles the "McDonalds" life style. _____

   _____

5. How does Luke 11:9 advise us to handle our "McDonald's" life style in relation to our Prayer

   life? _____

6. Think about what changes you need to make in your prayer life and note them

   here. _____

   _____

SECTION V:

STAND IN THE GAP

Ezekiel 22:30 "And I sought for a man among them, that should make up the hedge, and stand in the gap before me for the land, that I should not destroy it: but I found none."

When I think of standing in the gap I think of a huge space between me and my objective. If the space is big enough I might look at it as impossible to get through or around. At one time or another we have all been there. The objective can be anything, any goal. Healing, finances, emotional need, safety, a job, a home, and the list goes on. We know that somehow we must get to the other side. We are not sure what is between us and our objective, we just know we must get through, or around, that seemingly insurmountable obstacle blocking our way.

There are three areas involved here: A. The problem, B. the Gap, C. The other side (the answer). When we intercede for another our position is "B". We place ourselves in the gap between the problem and the answer. When we step into the gap we reach out to the problem and become a part of the answer through our prayers.

🏛 Who do you know, or what obstacles are you aware of, that needs someone to stand in the gap and pray? _____

Are you willing to step into the gap? _____

I remember many years ago when westerns were popular, there was a scene where the good guys came to a screeching "whoa" at the canyon entrance that was between them and their destination. It was a gap they had to get through, but first they wanted to know if there were any bad guys hiding in the rocks, ready to shoot them off their horses. One guy went ahead to check it out and make sure the others could make it through. He literally "stood in the gap", willing to accept whatever might be thrown at him for the safety and protection of his friends.

Are we willing to stand in the gap? A gap created by the sins of Adam and Eve, sins that we have perpetuated by living in disobedience and disbelief, sins that have created the gap between God and humanity.

Are we willing to suffer the hurt, the pain, the abuse, the loneliness, and the time it takes to intercede for a friend, an enemy, a pastor, a teacher, a neighbor we've never met, a lost and dying world? Are we willing to do battle with Satan, have our faith questioned and sometimes weakened? Are we willing to take on the burden of another, sharing their pain and suffering (physical or emotional)? It is a lot to think about and to consider. It is a decision only you can make, and one that only God can help you with.

🏛 After reading this paragraph do you sense your willingness faltering a little? How do you relate to the struggles and pain mentioned above? _____

_____

_____

_____

_____

The decision to "stand in the gap", to become an intercessor for the world around you, will be a decision you will never regret. It will be a decision that will bring you a glorious and indescribable closeness to God. A closeness that says, "I can sense His presence, His breath, His hand on me". Those are words that many people say but unfortunately many people have never felt. When you sense that closeness, when you know, and you know you know, those words are inadequate and sometimes you can only say "WOW".

God's presence brings peace, strength, contentment and a sense of separation from the world around you, as though you are wrapped in a cocoon of prayer. You sense the answer ready to burst forth, ready to display God's glory and splendor, releasing an energy of its own that speaks of God's greatness; a presence that overpowers the sinful world around us.

I like this definition of gap from Strong's Concordance:

GAP. (*E*zek. 22:30) perets (peh'-rets); Strong's #6556: "A break, breach; breaking forth."[15]

What is a gap if it not a breach, or a breaking forth, an opening, a gulf between two objects. If you look in any dictionary you will also see the word "gap" used as another word for breach. The visual picture for our study would be a large hole in a relationship between God and Man. Now picture you as the intercessor, stepping into that gap.

The following scriptures from the Word of God give God's perspective on what "standing in the gap" as an intercessor means:

Hebrews7:24-25 *"(24)But this man, because he continueth ever, hath an unchangeable priesthood. 25)Wherefore he is able also to save them to the uttermost that come unto God by him, seeing he ever liveth to make intercession for them."* (Christ stood in the greatest gap ever created – the gap between sinful man and the Father.)

Galatians 6:2 "Bear ye one another's burdens, and so fulfil the law of Christ." (When we stand in the gap for others we literally bear their burdens.)

Exodus 32:10, 11a, 14 "10) Now therefore let me alone, that my wrath may wax hot against them, and that I may consume them: and I will make of thee a great nation.11a) And Moses besought the LORD his God,.........14) And the LORD repented of the evil which he thought to do unto his people." (Moses stood in the gap pleading with God on behalf of the disobedient people God had brought out of the land of Egypt.)

I could name many examples of the results of intercessory prayer in my life, prayers that were answered because I just would not let go until God gave the answer (positive or negative). I have spent entire nights in fasting and prayer and entire days driving on long trips interceding on someone's behalf. I have spent weeks, months and years praying about a particular situation. I would pray until God placed the answer on my heart, or told me to move on without allowing the Holy Spirit to reveal the answer to me. Often the people involved do not realize I am praying. Their knowledge is not necessary, but by the Grace of God they will sense the prayer and know someone is lifting them up.

Who do you know right this minute that is in dire need of prayer and direction from God? _____

If not a person, what situation comes to mind? _____

_____

_____

I can look back on one such prayer that took place over 25 years ago. I knew a young man who believed he was called of God to preach and teach God's Word. The young man knew in his heart he wanted to be a pastor. He was encouraged to stay in his home church, take correspondence courses, and pursue his calling by staying put and working his way up through the ranks, until a pastor's position came available in his home church.

In my heart I believed this to be damaging to his growth and future leadership abilities. I felt the Holy Spirit guiding me in this thought pattern. I had nothing to gain or lose by his going off to school and nothing to gain or lose if he stayed. I sincerely believed the Holy Spirit was guiding me to pray about the situation. Could I have been wrong concerning this? Absolutely, but I knew if I were right the only way to turn the situation around was through prayer, and pray I did.

Like anyone else I began with morning and evening petitions to God, keeping the young man and his circumstances in God's presence. One evening the Holy Spirit impressed on my heart that what I needed to do was some old fashioned prayer and fasting. I purposed in my heart to follow the Holy Spirit's leading and began that evening. I began a vigil of prayer and fasting that night. I continued all through the next day and night until the following morning, a 36-hour fasting and prayer session. I struggled and pleaded with God on this young man's behalf. I pelted the heavens with my prayers. I prayed until my heart literally ached with the weight of this burden of prayer.

I am happy to say that in this case I did receive the answer and gained the knowledge that this young man would eventually go to Bible College. He did just that and went on to preach in another church where he prospered his congregation, the church, and him in the matters of God. And miraculously, after 25 years of growing and learning and gathering the experience and leadership abilities that God wanted for him, he was called to pastor his home church. He has gone full circle. Today he is serving and leading with a growth and maturity he gained from his experiences in his prior churches and in college.

Was this a result of just my prayer? I do not know. Was my intercession the final push needed to reach the young man's heart accomplishing God's purpose in this young man's life? Possibly, but I will never know this side of heaven. What I do know is the Holy Spirit uses us to reach the throne of grace - God's Grace. Will your prayer be the prayer that makes the difference? It well could be, but it definitely won't be if you do not intercede and pray.

Not every prayer will have such dramatic results. As I said before, often we will not know the results. Many times I've prayed my heart out and I was sure I felt God working, but God never revealed to me how He was working or what the result would be. I just knew I was to pray and that God would answer in His will, His way, and His time. Some things I have prayed for, and continue praying for, appear to be on the other side of the canyon. During those times it seems I cannot get past the canyon's entrance. My heart will not let me give up because I know that I cannot give up if the Holy Spirit is leading. Neither should you.

🏛 Why not stop right now and write a simple prayer asking God to make you the intercessory prayer warrior that He can use to enter the canyon entrance and let you be the one to stand in the gap? _____

_____

_____

_____

_____

The following story is told about Mr. D.L. Moody and is a wonderful picture of the power of Intercessory Prayer.

After the great Chicago fire Mr. Moody left for England for some well needed physical and spiritual refreshing. He left behind the ashes of what was once the church he preached at. The last thing in the world Mr. Moody wanted to do was preach. But being the well known man that he was he was immediately asked to fill the pulpit and deliver a sermon as only Mr. Moody could. He arrived at the church and as he stepped up to the pulpit all he could think of was, 'what a fool I was to consent to preach! I came here to listen, and here I am preaching.'

Mr. Moody had become, as so many of us do after a disaster befalls us, just worn out from the battle.

To continue the story Mr. Moody preached that morning to what he felt was a cold, icy audience and as he finished and peered out at the unmoving congregation it occurred to him he had also agreed to preach that night. His personal convictions would not allow him to do anything but keep his promise to preach that night. When he walked into the church there was an excitement that he had not felt that morning. After the sermon he gave an invitation for salvation and to his amazement five hundred people stood up wanting to receive Christ as their Savior. In shock he asked everyone sit down and did this three times. Each time five hundred people stood wanting to receive Christ.

What Mr. Moody did not know was that in the service that morning was the sister of an invalid woman who could not come. When she went home she told her sister about Mr. Moody being there. The invalid woman became excited and told how she had been praying for Mr. Moody to come to England and preach a great revival. She then excused herself to go and pray for the rest of the afternoon.

The faithful intercession of an invalid woman brought D.L. Moody to England and then brought 500 souls to Christ through his preaching. This invalid, who could not leave her home, found a special way to be used of God. She became an intercessor for the world around her. She stood in the gap that existed between God, Mr. Moody and the congregation. She stood in the gap that existed between London and God. She did not give up until God answered her prayer. If I close my eyes I can imagine this dear woman in a flat in London. Sick, unable to leave the house, her face glowing, she literally steps into that gap, bringing the Lord with her. Partnering with the Lord to put fire into Mr. Moody's preaching, resulting in 500 souls coming to a saving knowledge of the Lord Jesus Christ. What a powerful sight, a powerful witness and a powerful testimony of a person taking a burden and placing it at the feet of a most Holy and Powerful God.

Willingly standing in the gap and offering yourself up for hours and days at a time for the benefit of others is a difficult undertaking. It goes against the human inclination to lean towards selfish and self-centered pursuits that give us great personal benefit, yet does nothing to heighten another's position or status before the Lord or life in general.

The battle to walk away from self and step into someone else's circumstances is as great a battle as we ever want to undertake. Satan will step in with his most useful tool called "discouragement". He will point out all our faults and weaknesses and he will work at convincing us that we are wasting our time, that our prayer won't matter and who do you think you are anyway? Satan will put obstacles in our path trying to defeat us and cause us to stray from our purpose. Satan will try to block the entrance to the canyon with anything he can use to keep us from prayer.

The Holy Spirit can put a noose around Satan and clear the way for you to pray for the soul that has God placed on your heart, putting you in that gap that exists between the need and the answer.

I do not want to take away from our normal prayer time that we give to God. We may set aside 5, 10, 15, 20 minutes or more to pray, and often when we do that we try to place as many prayer requests into that block of time as we can. Please do not misunderstand me, I do not wish to imply that this is wrong. Please continue to set aside that block of time and continue to go through your list of prayer requests as you have always done. It is an important part of petitioning God for the needs of others, as well as for our own needs, a time devoted to keeping something or someone's name constantly before the throne of grace.

What I am trying to stress throughout this work is that standing in the gap for a special need is separate from your normal prayer time; it is an entirely different way of approaching God. It is a bombardment on God to give special attention to a need presented to you by the Holy Spirit. This does not mean that God is not concerned about the spontaneous utterances brought to Him. He cares about all our needs, no matter how we bring them to Him. The emphasis here is on the need to set aside a special time, a "gap standing" time if you will, a time to intercede for just one particular circumstance with all your heart. A time devoted to giving all your energy to the task of reaching God, placing that particular need at the feet of Jesus and praying until you are aware of God's presence and have the sense of hearing God's answer.

I cannot stress strongly enough the importance of having a mindset that leads us to "stand in the gap" and to be the intercessor between the person, or circumstances we are praying for, and God. With such a mind-set we will not only be willing to pray, we will not be able to stop ourselves from praying.

There will be times when we start praying and we may not have any idea what we are going to say or how we will start. During those times the Holy Spirit will step in and give us the introduction we need to enter heavens realm with our prayer. He will give us the direction and guidance we need.

🏛 Can you recall a time when you started to pray and the words just would not come? Look up Romans 8:26 and write it here. _____

_____

_____

As our prayer flows from our heart, through the power of the Holy Spirit, we will find the right words to present our petition to a loving and caring God. There may be times when we find ourselves limited in time because we must go to work, or school, or an appointment, or whatever, but our heart is not ready to let the prayer go and say amen. During these times we learn the true meaning of *I Thessalonians 5:16-17 ¹⁶⁾Rejoice evermore, ¹⁷⁾ pray without ceasing,"*

It doesn't matter what you are doing throughout the day, your prayer continues to replay itself and you have an overwhelming compulsion to continue petitioning God for that need.

I get so excited just typing this because I know the continual petitioning of God is exciting. Whether on your knees, walking, doing dishes, working, or at every break in the momentum of the day, the prayer continues. Constantly being in touch with God is one of the most comforting, peaceful, and rewarding experiences we can have, even at life's most hectic times.

I wish I could promise you that it would always be like that, but I can't. As the saying goes "life happens". Satan's interference happens and human imperfections happen. I do know this however, the more time we spend with God the more resistance we can expect from Satan, yet at the same time we will also begin to grow closer to God. Satan will urge you to quit but you will be able to lean on the power of the Holy Spirit that is working within you, giving you the strength to carry on.

As I sit writing this I know Satan is at work. He is trying to push aside the presence of the Holy Spirit and is trying to squash my desire for godly pursuits. Satan is whispering in my ear telling me that none of this is going to help anyone, no one is going to like this Bible study, and no one will want to read what I have written.

Satan does not want us to spend extra time in prayer, to stand in the gap, interceding for others. Satan would rather we were all milk-toast Christians that take the easy way out. Satan does not mind that we are Christians as long as we are not praying Christians. It is Satan's wish that we keep our thoughts to ourselves, sit down, lie down and shut up!!! But definitely don't stand up, look up, or speak up for God and to God. Satan wants to play in our fields and destroy our harvest. We must continue the fight, stand in the gap, look up to our Lord, and push Satan aside.

Praise God that Christ stood in the gap for us, that Christ bore our sin and shame and filled the gap between man and God. Through all our trials and tribulations we can be secure in the knowledge that Christ, and Christ alone, filled a gap we could never fill. Christ is our lookout. He has gone ahead of us. Christ's crucifixion allows us to pass through our canyon of sin and escape the ambush that would surely send us to hell.

The Blood of Jesus has flowed into, and filled, the gap that existed between man and God; the ultimate gap, the gap of sin and shame. Now it is our turn to stand in the gaps that open between God and man. As human beings we fall short (it will always be that way) and we will always need a boost to get us on the right track. Without that boost we cannot live an effective Christian life, serving God to the fullest. As we stand in the gap for others, others will do the same for us, empowering us to continue our prayer march to the heavenlies.

How blessed we are to be so in tune with God that He gives us a glimpse forward to a time when we will always be in tune with Him. That day will come when we stand face-to-face with our loving Lord and Savior.

🏛 Has God revealed to you how you can be a "Stand in the Gap" intercessory prayer warrior? Who or what has He laid on your heart? _____

_____

_____

Closing Moments

1. When we intercede for another person what is our position? _____

   _____

2. What does God's presence bring us?_____

   _____

3. How can you apply the story of D.L. Moody to your life? First try to relate to Mr. Moody's

   emotional state and then try to relate to the invalid woman who prayed? _____

   _____

   _____

4. When we pray who is our Intercessor? _____

5. I Thessalonians 5:17 tells us to? _____ _____ _____

6. The ultimate gap has been filled for us by whom? _____

SECTION VI:

PRAYING GOD'S WILL

Genesis 18: 22-29, 32-33) "(22)And the men turned their faces from thence, and went toward Sodom: but Abraham stood yet before the LORD. (23)And Abraham drew near, and said, Wilt thou also destroy the righteous with the wicked? (24)Peradventure there be fifty righteous within the city: wilt thou also destroy and not spare the place for the fifty righteous that are therein? (25)That be far from thee to do after this manner, to slay the righteous with the wicked: and that the righteous should be as the wicked, that be far from thee: Shall not the Judge of all the earth do right? (26)And the LORD said, If I find in Sodom fifty righteous within the city, then I will spare all the place for their sakes. (27)And Abraham answered and said, Behold now, I have taken upon me to speak unto the LORD, which am but dust and ashes: (28)Peradventure there shall lack five of the fifty righteous: wilt thou destroy all the city for lack of five? And he said, If I find there forty and five, I will not destroy it. (29)And he spake unto him yet again, and said, Peradventure there shall be forty found there. And he said, I will not do it for forty's sake…………. (32)And he said, Oh let not the LORD be angry, and I will speak yet but this once: Peradventure ten shall be found there. And he said, I will not destroy it for ten's sake. (33)And the LORD went his way, as soon as he had left communing with Abraham: and Abraham returned unto his place."

"Father, please answer this if it be your will and your way." How many times have we prayed for someone and said those words, or something similar. Not praying specifically that God would answer our prayer, only if it is His will and His way, often not believing He will answer our prayer. Most of our prayers are one time petitions and we do not pray through to the end expecting results. We receive requests during prayer meeting or from a friend, we offer up the need, and then move on to other requests. Please do not misunderstand, I am all for prayer meetings and personal requests. I believe God answers many of those prayers, but there are times when we need to pray through until we see the answer.

We want God's will and way in our lives and in the lives of all whom we pray for. But we must be careful that we do not use that phrase as a cop-out, an excuse not to pray specifically, simply because we do not have enough faith to believe that God can and does answer specific prayers. I know there are times when we are praying for someone and we don't know how to pray, or what to pray, maybe an unspoken request, or just a name placed on your heart. At those times there are almost no other words to pray except "God please have your will and your way in whatever the circumstance might be".

I want to present two possible scenarios based on the scripture above, although I am sure some enterprising soul can think up more than these two, but I will only address two possible scenarios:

Scenario Number 1: It was God's will that Sodom and Gomorrah be destroyed. Abraham was just praying into the wind, hoping that maybe, just maybe, God would change His mind. God allowed Abraham to bargain with Him just to pacify Abraham. God never intended to change His mind. In the end Sodom and Gomorrah were destroyed, the destruction itself would lend credence to this argument.

Scenario No. 2: Abraham knew something we have yet to learn. God can and does change His mind because of the prayers of the righteous. The result must be to the Glory of God and not just to satisfy our personal needs. God always provides for our needs. Had He chosen to save Sodom and Gomorrah it would have been to glorify God, not Abraham, not Sodom and Gomorrah, only God. Had there been ten righteous men God promised He would spare Sodom and Gomorrah, and for His Glory He would have, but there were not ten to be found.

I subscribe to Scenario Number 2 because I believe God is in the business of answering the prayers of a righteous man. As I said before, God does not always answer our prayers exactly to our specifications, but I believe God can, and does, step back from His original intent if His Glory will be magnified. When God chooses not to answer our specific request I believe it simply means God's greater glory will be accomplished another way. The key to praying God's will is to put ourselves and our personal wishes aside. I hope this idea will become clearer by the time we finish this section.

🏛 Which of these two scenarios' do you subscribe to?_____

Why?_____

_____

_____

Our basic problem is we do not trust God to make the right choice. We do not believe God has acted in our best interest when He answers our prayers contrary to what we asked. We should take to heart the title of an old TV show "Father Knows Best". As Christians we could the show to match how our heart should believe, "Father God Knows Best".

The most difficult prayer is the prayer for healing. You may pray your heart and soul into exhaustion, yet your loved one still dies. Why? In your heart you know there is an evil person who has lived through worse, so why take a good man or woman from this earth? Why? Deuteronomy 29:29 says: ***"The secret things belong to the LORD our God,..."*** We must have faith that God is acting in our best interest and for His glory and honor. "Father God Knows Best".

We mentioned that God is in the business of answering the prayers of a righteous man. Do we fall into the category of a righteous man or woman? Just what is righteous?

Merriam-Webster Online Dictionary defines Righteous as: *acting in accord with divine or moral law; free from guilt or sin ...*[16]

"Free from guilt" is only possible by laying your heart open before a true and living God who has promised us forgiveness through His Son. First and foremost we must be free from the guilt of sin and shame, which is brought about through our personal relationship with Christ. Have we accepted Christ as our Savior? Did we then, and do we now, continually ask God's forgiveness of sin? If our answer to both these questions is yes, then we can honestly say we fit this part of the definition "free from guilt". Once we have been forgiven we no longer need to carry the burden of guilt.

> *Romans 3:23 "For all have sinned, and come short of the glory of God;"*
>
> *Romans 5:8 "But God commendeth his love toward us, in that, while we were yet sinners, Christ died for us."*
>
> *Colossians 1:14 "In whom we have redemption through his blood, even the forgiveness of sins:"*

"Acting in accord with divine or moral law" can be accomplished if we not only read God's Word, but do our utmost to live God's Word. We need to follow His commandments, allowing God to live through us. Saved and sanctified, righteous in the eyes of God, just as Abraham was.

> *Acts 26:18: "To open their eyes, and to turn them from darkness to light, and from the power of Satan unto God, that they may receive forgiveness of sins, and inheritance among them which are sanctified by faith that is in me."*

Now we are in the position to fulfill the scripture verse below:

James 5:16 "Confess your faults one to another, and pray one for another, that ye may be healed. The effectual fervent prayer of a righteous man availeth much."

🏛 After reading the definitions above do you consider yourself a righteous person?

_____

If not, stop and pray and ask God to help you see His righteousness in you and help you to realize your own righteousness through Him.

Please keep in mind there is a difference between a righteous person and a self-righteous person. We saw the definition of righteous above, but a self-righteous person is defined in the Merriam-Webster Online Dictionary as: *"convinced of one's own righteousness especially in contrast with the actions and beliefs of others: narrow-mindedly moralistic."*[17] A self-righteous person does not act in accord with God's divine law. A self-righteous person is a law unto himself or herself, thinking himself or herself above all others and better than all others, with no real need for the one true God of heaven. The self-righteous person has made himself or herself a God unto themselves.

When we begin to believe only our prayers are effective we have stepped into the realm of the self-righteous. We must not allow ourselves to be filled with pride when we see answers to our prayers, remember there are many others praying as well. Conversely we cannot go into prayer with a lackadaisical attitude either, an attitude that says "my prayer won't matter others are praying anyway". There may be times when others are not praying and you are the only one praying in a specific way. You have no way of knowing whether that is the case or not. Therefore you should pray with all your heart, as if you are the only one praying, but not be so vain that you believe you are the only one God hears.

I have just been through a prayer time with God that shed new light on this section. I struggled not only with self-righteousness in prayer, but the commonality of the expression "If it be thy will Lord, I ask that…." It seems like such a worn out, well used phrase, and yet it contains the kernels of truth that we get from the Word of God about praying the will of God.

I have struggled with how to approach this topic and allow for a clearer understanding of that phrase and the truth of it. This morning I believe God pointed out some important truths to me by reminding me of some things that occurred during my intercessory prayer for a man who was suffering and, by the doctors own reports, was terminal.

I had entered into prayer with my prayer partner one morning with a deep burden to pray for a certain man and his family. I don't wish to intrude on the family's privacy or into their grief so I will fictitiously name the man "Daniel" after that solid Bible character who I believe represents the character of the man I prayed for.

I went to my prayer partner's house with such a deep burden for Daniel. I told her that I believed we should intercede for Daniel because his disease was eating away at his body. We prayed and wept and I even fasted all day, hoping to shore up my prayer and really show God my sincerity, my belief that this man should be spared. I prayed, that like Hezekiah in Isaiah 38:1-8 and II Kings 20:1-6, God would give Daniel 15 more years. I prayed God would extend Daniel's life with health and happiness, allowing him more time on earth to serve God and more time for his family as well. I knew Daniel was a man who loved God and served him in and out of the church and by human reasoning he deserved to live, but it was not to be so.

Let me interject here that our ways are not God's ways and our human reasoning does not take precedence over God's will and God's plan for humanity. While we are searching for God's reasoning we tend to interject our own reasoning, our human reasoning. God is not required to give a reason for what He does. We need to believe that what God does will ultimately be for God's glory and ultimately for our good.

Back to the story, I kept praying daily, on some days longer than others, that God would extend Daniel's life just as he did Hezekiah's life. I tried to convince myself that God's will and God's plan was to physically heal Daniel and extend his life here on earth. My goodness, I was praying God's Word for the man, at the same time telling myself it was God's will. Yet down in the depths of my heart there was a nagging, prickly sensation that I was missing something.

When I got word that they had called in hospice I checked and found they only gave Daniel one week at the most to live. The disease was popping up all over his body. I grieved quietly and prayed quietly. I felt confusion and disappointment. Wouldn't that have been a miraculous example of God's glory and grace, His mercy and His power, if Daniel, a man given up for dead, had lived, Wow! But it was not to be.

I could not impose my own self righteousness, no matter how good my intentions, on God's righteousness. I could not impose my will onto God's will. For some reason God had decided that stepping back, repenting of His original plan for Daniel, would not bring Him as much Glory, would not magnify Him as much as taking Daniel home to Glory. I will never know this side of glory, why God made this choice. I can only trust God and continue to pray as He would guide and direct.

My special prayer this morning was for Daniel and his family, to grieve with God on their behalf, and to question God about why I felt the need to pray as I had and Daniel's life was not extended. As I was praying God reminded me of the day when I had prayed with my prayer partner especially for Daniel. God reminded me of just that moment in my prayer when I said to God, "I know God, I know, but I am still going to pray this way, pray that he is healed". Truthfully, I knew at that moment God's will for Daniel, I just did not want to accept it. I wanted to believe that this was one of those times when God would be willing to step back, all for the Glory of God of course. I remembered the nagging, prickly sensation I had and now I knew what it was. I was not obedient. I failed to listen to God's direction.

⚏ Recall a time when you felt a nagging, prickly sensation, and ignored it. Record that moment here and refer to it as a reminder of the need for unquestioned obedience to God in your prayer life?_____

_____

_____

_____

God does reveal to us His will while we are in prayer, as well as revealing His will through His Word. When I continued to pray for Daniel's healing and extended life I had quit praying God's Will. I willed myself not to believe what God had told me during prayer because I did not want it to be true. And therein rests the problem of humanity. We want what we want and disguise our wants as prayer. A horribly pious approach to the throne of Grace don't you think? I wish I was not guilty of such pious behavior but obviously I am. I just confessed as much.

What does this illustration teach us? Here are my firsthand observations:

1. God's will is revealed through His Word

2. God's will is revealed through our prayers

3. We must listen when God speaks, even when the message is hard to take.

4. We can pray for someone, or something, and even if human eye finds the situation hopeless *Mark 10:27 applies: "And Jesus looking upon them saith, With men it is impossible, but not with God: for with God all things are possible."*

5. Until we pray with sincerity, not for others to hear, but in our heart of hearts, we will never recognize God's possibilities for our lives, or the lives of others.

6. Intercessory prayer is hard and it can hurt. It makes the heart ache. It makes the heart jump for joy. We will have both the hard to accept revelations, as well as the good revelations that are easier to accept.

7. We can never give up on God's wisdom or try to supersede it: we must accept His wisdom above our own.

8. God's timing is always perfect: we may not be able to grasp the perfection of His timing.

9. God's will is always perfect, despite human resistance to God's will.

10. We may make mistakes in discerning God's will but we must learn from our mistakes and not let Satan get the victory by using his most effective tool: discouragement.

Can you add to the list of lessons learned from your own experiences?_____

_____

_____

God used Daniel not only as an effective tool and witness for God through his life, but also in his death. Daniel died just as the doctors had predicted, within a week. God let me go through all this now because He knew exactly when Daniel was going to go home to eternity to rule and reign with his heavenly Father. He knew when that time of everlasting rest and ever-lasting healing would take place. Daniel's testimony lives on through this story and through his family. No greater tribute can I pay him than by including one of his final contributions to God's work on earth in this book.

You may wonder who Daniel is but his true identity is not as important as the lessons we can learn from this experience. To whom does the glory and honor belong, Daniel would say it all belongs to God. To God be the Glory.

Now we have come full circle and you may be thinking, so why didn't you just pray, "if it's your will, heal" in the first place. First, I did not know God's will until I prayed. Second, I would never have known God's will if all I said was, "If it's your will, heal". God could easily have led me to pray His will for earthly healing, had that been His will. Had I accepted what

God said in the beginning I would have prayed differently, and I would have been praying God's will. All this only makes me stronger in my belief that God does speak to us, we just don't always listen.

***Romans 8:26- 27** "(26)Likewise the Spirit also helpeth our infirmities: for we know not what we should pray for as we ought: but the Spirit itself maketh intercession for us with groanings which cannot be uttered. (27)And he that searcheth the hearts knoweth what is the mind of the Spirit, because he maketh intercession for the saints according to the will of God."*

I am certain that throughout this entire time, throughout this struggle, the Holy Spirit was interceding on my behalf and praying the will of God for Daniel's life.

We might also ask: Why does God need us to pray His will? God most certainly can attend to the matter without us. It is difficult to put into words the excitement that comes into your heart when God uses you as His "right hand person" by allowing you to pelt the heavens with prayer. He allows you to fight satanic forces, opening the gap that allows the love, comfort, grace, mercy and hope of God to shine through. Also, the knowledge that if it will ultimately project God's glory to other's, God can, and has, changed His path, His direction and honored the prayers of a righteous and sincere man.

***Numbers 14:15-16, 20-21** "(15)Now if thou shalt kill all this people as one man, then the nations which have heard the fame of thee will speak, saying, (16)Because the LORD was not able to bring this people into the land which he sware unto them, therefore he hath slain them in the wilderness."*

As I understand this passage God was ready to, and it was His will to, destroy the people because of their disobedience and rejection of Him, yet Moses prayed that God would reverse His stand, reverse His will in the matter. How bold can a man get, quite bold it seems, and it leads me to believe that God expects the same boldness in prayer from us. God could have easily let Moses know that he would not change His mind and devastation would follow, but that is not how the story played out.

Numbers 14:20-21.[20] *And the LORD said, I have pardoned according to thy word:* [21]*But as truly as I live, all the earth shall be filled with the glory of the LORD."*

This should give us all assurance that prayer is not just a futile exercise in which we have no power. Our power is given to us by God. God's Word is full of wonderful and exciting stories that illustrate and confirm the powerful relationship we can have with God. Let's take a look at the story of Hannah.

Clearly Hannah believed herself to be barren with no likelihood of ever having children. Her husband Elkanah loved her but he too felt she would never be able to bear him a child:

I Samuel 1:5 "But unto Hannah he gave a worthy portion; for he loved Hannah: but the LORD had shut up her womb."

Year after year Hannah would go to the house of the Lord and pray for a child. Through it all Elkanah loved Hannah and tried to comfort her but that was not enough, Hannah wanted a child. To make matters worse Elkanah's other wife taunted her and made fun because she had many sons and Hannah had none.

I Samuel 1:9-11 "⁹⁾ So Hannah rose up after they had eaten in Shiloh, and after they had drunk. Now Eli the priest sat upon a seat by a post of the temple of the LORD. ¹⁰⁾And she was in bitterness of soul, and prayed unto the LORD, and wept sore. ¹¹⁾And she vowed a vow, and said, O LORD of hosts, if thou wilt indeed look on the affliction of thine handmaid, and remember me, and not forget thine handmaid, but wilt give unto thine handmaid a man child, then I will give him unto the LORD all the days of his life, and there shall no razor come upon his head."

All the evidence points to Hannah's womb being closed but she prayed and prayed and finally made her agreement with God as we just read in I Samuel 1:9-11 above. What had seemed like an insurmountable hurdle, and definitely one she could not change on her own, became an answered prayer. Hannah would bare a son.

Did Hannah's prayer change God's mind? Had Hannah not prayed so desperately, believing God would change His mind and open her womb, do you believe she would still have had a child because it was "ultimately' the will of God? Why did God close her womb and then open it after years of prayer, and then only after she made her agreement? Was it in response to Hannah's faith in God? Was it because all along God wanted Hannah to have Samuel and allow him to be raised by the priests? Was it because the greater Glory was in Hannah being barren and having a child only because of her prayer so we could be beneficiaries of this witness and testimony all these many centuries later?

🏛 Answer these questions based on this study and your personal study of the Word of God.

_____

_____

_____

Whatever your answers the one thing we know for a certainty is that God wants us to pray, not to quit unless the Holy Spirit directs us to stop praying or redirects our prayer. We could miss the blessing that God has for us if we gloss over the true power of prayer, even in seemingly impossible circumstances. Even more devastating would be for us to miss true fellowship and friendship with God because we failed to talk to Him.

Moses and Hannah, two very different illustrations and yet they have the same ending. God's will was done and the prayers of His saints were necessary for their interaction with God and their fellowship with God. There are many other examples of biblical prayers, below are just a few more.

Exodus 32:11-14 "[11] And Moses besought the LORD his God, and said, LORD, why doth thy wrath wax hot against thy people, which thou hast brought forth out of the land of Egypt with great power, and with a mighty hand? [12]Wherefore should the Egyptians speak, and say, For mischief did he bring them out, to slay them in the mountains, and to consume them from the face of the earth? Turn from thy fierce wrath, and repent of this evil against thy people. [13]Remember Abraham, Isaac, and Israel, thy servants, to whom thou swarest by thine own self, and saidst unto them, I will multiply your seed as the stars of heaven, and all this land that I have spoken of will I give unto your seed, and they shall inherit it for ever. [14]And the LORD repented of the evil which he thought to do unto his people."

Jeremiah 26:18-19 "[18]Micah the Morasthite prophesied in the days of Hezekiah king of Judah, and spake to all the people of Judah, saying, Thus saith the LORD of hosts; Zion shall be plowed like a field, and Jerusalem shall become heaps, and the mountain of the house as the high places of a forest. [19]Did Hezekiah king of Judah and all Judah put him at all to death? did he not fear the LORD, and besought the

LORD, and the LORD repented him of the evil which he had pronounced against them? Thus might we procure great evil against our souls."

Amos 7:2-6 "[2]And it came to pass, that when they had made an end of eating the grass of the land, then I said, O Lord GOD, forgive, I beseech thee: by whom shall Jacob arise? for he is small. [3]The LORD repented for this: It shall not be, saith the LORD. [4]Thus hath the Lord GOD shewed unto me: and, behold, the Lord GOD called to contend by fire, and it devoured the great deep, and did eat up a part. [5]Then said I, O Lord GOD, cease, I beseech thee: by whom shall Jacob arise? for he is small. [6]The LORD repented for this: This also shall not be, saith the Lord GOD."

Before I close this section I wish to cover one final thought on praying the will of God. I was asked what about the famous passage in the New Testament where Jesus prays that God's will be done:

Matthew 26:39: "And he went a little farther, and fell on his face, and prayed, saying, O my Father, if it be possible, let this cup pass from me: nevertheless not as I will, but as thou wilt."

I am not a theologian so I will not try to give a long theological dissertation about this passage. I will simply share with you what I believe was happening here, which I guess is as good as any Doctor of Theology since theology is man's reasoning of God's Word. Let's go back a few verses and pick up at Matthew 26:36 read through to verse 39 in context.   *"[36]Then cometh Jesus with them unto a place called Gethsemane, and saith unto the disciples, Sit ye here, while I go and pray yonder. [37]And he took with him Peter and the two sons of Zebedee, and began to be sorrowful and very heavy. [38]Then saith he unto them, My soul is exceeding sorrowful, even unto death: tarry ye here, and watch with me. [39]And he went a little farther, and fell on his face, and prayed, saying, O my Father, if it be possible, let this cup pass from me: nevertheless not as I will, but as thou wilt."*

Jesus set out to pray because He knew the next major event in his life was The Cross. Did God reveal to His son that He was going to die and His death would be for the sins of humanity, and that's why He needed to go to Gethsemane to pray? Did God reveal only parts of His plan to His son, Jesus? Was it after Jesus said to His Father, "if it is possible, let this cup pass from me" that He suddenly felt the Holy Spirit revealing His impending death? Is that why the next portion of the prayer is, "nevertheless, not as I will, but as you will"?

Step one: ask. Step two: listen. Step three: respond. 1. Jesus prayed for His life. 2. Jesus heard the answer. 3. Jesus began praying God's will. Could God have changed His mind because of that prayer? Absolutely, but to change His mind in that instance would not have allowed God's glory to shine through in your life and mine.

Consider that had human reasoning prevailed the prayer would have gone something like "He's a good man Lord, look at all the good He can do for God. Leave him here God to serve you for the betterment of mankind". Had human reasoning taken over we would have been followers of evil with no hope for our soul. I have a friend who made me a plaque of her favorite saying, and it applies here. It simply says: "Ain't it Great". It sure is, because God, through His son Jesus Christ, made it great for us.

In closing this section I want to tie in praying God's word with praying His will. The following scriptures are an introduction to praying God's Word in that they teach us to keep His Word close to our heart, be open to the teaching of His Word, and to continually meditate on His Word. When we can't seem to find the right words the Holy Spirit can use the Word of God to guide us in our prayer and to teach us how to pray.

Psalm 119:11-12, 18, 97 [11] *Thy word have I hid in mine heart, that I might not sin against thee.* [12] *Blessed art thou, O LORD: teach me thy statutes....* [18] *Open thou mine eyes, that I may behold wondrous things out of thy law… [97] O how love I thy law! it is my meditation all the day."*

You notice how throughout this study I have used scriptures to emphasize an action or a direction, to guide us as we go. All of that is part of praying God's Word. We gain knowledge of God and how He wants us to pray and in which direction to go based on His Word. Below are other scriptures that reflect praying God's Word:

Psalm 51:10 "Create in me a clean heart, O God; and renew a right spirit within me." (That I might come before you, presenting my petitions in wholesome cleanliness.)

Hebrews 12:1 "Wherefore seeing we also are compassed about with so great a cloud of witnesses, let us lay aside every weight, and the sin which doth so easily beset us, and let us run with patience the race that is set before us," (Help me shake out the cob webs of my mind and heart and present my petitions with a pure and holy heart)

Galatians 6:2 "Bear ye one another's burdens, and so fulfil the law of Christ." (Lord help me carry the burden as I pray, transferring their burden to me. Ease their pain Lord.)

It is impossible to pray God's will if we have not prepared ourselves by praying God's Word for our condition. We must come before God only after we have had a cleansing bath, scrubbed and rinsed in the Word of God.

   Stop now and pray God's Word for your life as an Intercessory Prayer Warrior. Use the scriptures above to help get you started. What are some other scriptures you can think of that will help you in your preparations for Holy and righteous prayer? _____

_____

_____

Closing Moments

1. Do you think that you could have had an Abraham faith without the written Word of God at your side? Why or why not? _____

   _____

2. The most difficult prayer is the prayer for _____?

   Why do you think that is?_____

   _____

3. What does Deuteronomy 29:29 say? _____

   _____

4. How do you balance Merriam Webster's definition of righteous and Romans 3:23? ___

   _____

   _____

5. What are your thoughts on praying the will of God?_____

   _____

   _____

6. How does your answer above reconcile with Numbers 14:15-21? _____

   _____

SECTION VII:

CONFIDENCE AND PASSION IN PRAYER

Psalm 5:1-3 ¹⁾Give ear to my words, O LORD, consider my meditation. ²⁾Hearken unto the voice of my cry, my King, and my God: for unto thee will I pray. ³⁾My voice shalt thou hear in the morning, O LORD; in the morning will I direct my prayer unto thee, and will look up."

This morning I received an E-Mail containing a group of pictures that reflected a mountain in Japan whose peak was well above the land below. Although it did not give the height of the mountain, the photo from the top looking down revealed the detail, or lack of detail, usually seen from an aircraft. The photos showed people going up the side of the mountain on a man made walk that consisted mainly of two or three boards that looked like 2X6 planks. The planks were tied together with some type of steel staples anchored into the mountainside with chain and spikes. A chain handrail was spiked into the side of the mountain to use as a handhold while climbing. The footing was precarious to say the least. You could see the people walking on the planks, walking in a circular manner around and up the mountain. Mountain goats walk around and around a mountain from the bottom to the top in a circular manner to keep their balance. This was the same principle.

I cannot imagine taking on such a climb. I would have absolutely no passion for that type of an adventure and I would definitely lack confidence in my ability to make it to the top. I'm the type of person who cannot look out a window if I'm more than a few floors up. My stomach churns, my throat constricts, and my body stiffens in anticipation of what could happen. I might be able to take a step or two but I am sure that would be the end of the adventure for me. I do not especially like heights.

That mountain is like our prayer life. We come to the beginning of the climb and at that moment we make a decision about our ability to achieve the climb and our desire, or our passion, for the effort it would take to carry out the feat. We can develop thoughts of fear in our prayer life, either fear that our prayers will not be answered or fear that if they are answered we will be obligated to greater service to God. As a consequence we sometimes give lip service, not prayer service, during our prayer time. We can let fear stop us from an effective and fruitful prayer life just like I would let fear keep me from climbing that mountain (it's a psychological fear, not a fear of death).

Looking at the pictures of the mountain and the scene below, I know if I reached the top it would be a beautiful, picturesque sight and well worth the climb, but still the courage and determination are missing. Because I lack confidence in my ability I cannot develop a passion for the adventure. As a result I will never see the scene from the top of the mountain and I can only imagine what it would look like. How sad that often that is exactly how our prayer life is. We can only imagine what it is like to sense God's peace and presence, to know His power and might, simply because we do not have the confidence and the passion for prayer that allows us to accept the challenge. We call on God with a need, we might even plead a little, but then we move on. We lack the determination and passion necessary to keep climbing up our mountain of prayer. Sometimes it is good to lay your petition at the feet of Jesus during the first request and then move on. The key is to know when to move on. Are you willing to keep on praying for a particular need until God releases the burden from your soul? Are you willing to accept the burden to begin with? We must be careful not to approach prayer with our McDonald's life-style attitude that we mentioned in Section IV. Give me a Big Mac, fries, a shake and I'm out of here. Make Suzy well, give John Boy a job, Gertrude a husband and I'm out of here. Ouch! How many times have I been guilty of just that?

- 🏛 Do a quick assessment of your prayer life. Do you find there are times when you are guilty of the "McDonald" approach to prayer? _____

- 🏛 Write out a short prayer asking God to help you avoid the rushed and hurried prayers that are synonymous with our face paced lifestyle today?_____

_____

_____

_____

Our approach to prayer should be one of excitement and our attitude one of confidence. Are you excited? Are you confident in your relationship with God? Do you have a passion for prayer that surpasses your passion for your favorite pastime or your passion for your family? Do you, in the depth of your heart and soul, believe God hears and will answer your prayer? If so, you must step out with confidence. Approach God with boldness, get up close and personal, not in a hurry, but with a calmness and desire that exudes your confidence in God's desire to hear and answer prayer.

I placed the following definitions in tandem because I don't believe we will ever develop a passion for prayer if we do not have the confidence we need to approach God with faith and belief.

Confidence: **a:** a feeling or consciousness of one's powers or of reliance on one's circumstances **b:** faith or belief that one will act in a right, proper, or effective way <have *confidence* in a leader>...[18]

<u>Passion</u>: Etymology: from Latin *pati* to suffer: … [4b)]intense, driving, or overmastering feeling or conviction:…[19]

In the definitions above you will notice that first we must recognize our own power and then have faith in that power and our ability to use our power effectively in prayer. At first glance that sounds a bit self-righteous and self-centered, but if we stop and think about it we realize we do not get this power of our own volition or by our own ability to produce the power. We can only attain this power through God. Without God we are powerless. The last part of the definition of confidence says "confidence in a leader". We must let God be our leader and trust him to give us what we need. Our self-reliance might well be our downfall. We have become such a high tech society, with gadget upon gadget available to provide our every need that we forget that before gadgets there was God. We need to trust God for "prayer power" and trust prayer to get us through the rough and tough times. Let's lay down our gadgets and turn to God.

What are some of the gadgets you depend on to get you through your daily routines?

_____

_____

_____

_____

Currently I am using a computer to type this and listening to praise worship on the radio as I type. Could I do without these to carry out this task? Could God give me the strength to write this by hand, hearing only the music of his presence to encourage me? Of course I could, but thank God he allowed someone to invent the computer. The problem arises if I let my gadgets take the place of my relationship with God?

Interestingly, in the definition of passion you will notice the word is derived from the Latin word "Pati", to suffer. Prayer can be such a heavy burden that we can suffer under the weight of that load. It is that suffering that gives us our drive, our intense need, our need to shed ourselves of the burden and give that burden to God. Have you ever watched weight lifters, they start small and work their way up to heavier and heavier weights until the load is so great they need a spotter to help lay the weight down. Imagine those weights as the burdens you carry in prayer and Christ as your spotter, the one who helps you lay your burdens down. Just as a weight lifter needs a spotter, we need Christ.

We should carry these burdens to our prayer closet with excitement and passion. Without that excitement and passion for prayer we will be sluggish and dutiful in our approach to God, which does not lend itself to a confident, powerful approach to His throne of grace. What do you think would happen if our weight lifter in the example above became sluggish and unenthusiastic? What a crushing experience that would be. Our prayers also suffer crushing experiences under the weight of sluggishness and lack-luster enthusiasm. Dr. Jack Hyles preached a sermon entitled "Duty". Dr Hyles pointed out that we often pray about things that God has already told us to do. Prayer is one of those things God asks of you. God tells us to pray in I Thessalonians 5:17 where Paul wrote: *"pray without ceasing"*. Prayer is our duty, but if all we do is think of prayer as a duty, prayer will become nothing more than vain words and vain repetitions offered up without emotions or meaning. Yes it is your duty to pray, but God expects you to put your heart and soul into your prayers. The more focused on God that you are, the more committed you are to prayer, the more confident you become. The following scriptures give us many examples of confidence in prayer.

1 John 5:14 "And this is the confidence that we have in him, that, if we ask any thing according to his will, he heareth us:"

Eph 3:12 "In whom we have boldness and access with confidence by the faith of him."

II Tim 1:12 "For the which cause I also suffer these things: nevertheless I am not ashamed: for I know whom I have believed, and am persuaded that he is able to keep that which I have committed unto him against that day."

Philippians 1:6 "Being confident of this very thing, that he which hath begun a good work in you will perform it until the day of Jesus Christ:"

Hebrews 10:35 "Cast not away therefore your confidence, which hath great recompence of reward."

So much in the scriptures tells us to be confident. When we have confidence we will pray with a passion predicated on our belief that God can and will answer our prayers.

Stop and think about your approach to prayer. Do you pray with confidence? Write an assessment of your confidence in prayer._____

_____

_____

In defining confidence did you also notice that it made reference to our faith or belief in our leader? In this case God is our leader. Below is a definition of faith that intertwines all the necessary ingredients for a confident, productive prayer life.

"Faith: **1 a** (1): belief and trust in and loyalty to God (2): belief in the traditional doctrines of a religion **b** (1): firm belief in something for which there is no proof (2): complete trust **2**: something that is believed especially with strong conviction; *especially*: a system of religious beliefs <the Protestant *faith*>"[20]

It is the strength of our faith that provides the cornerstone and the foundation for a strong, confident and passionate prayer life. What a struggle to elaborate on the confidence and passion we need in our prayer life. Sometimes prayer is so exciting it makes me want to jump up and down and lift my voice in Holy Hallelujahs. At other times the need for prayer becomes a burden so heavy it makes my heart literally ache.

It is during the burdensome prayers, the ones that make your heart ache, that we need the greatest faith and confidence. It is during those times that we must remember where our confidence comes from, and in whom we must place our trust. It is God, and God alone, in whom we must place our trust and our faith. Satan will explore our minds and watch our daily actions to try to find a weak point, to find the most minuscule fragment of doubt. When Satan finds that doubt he will use it as a foothold to wiggle his way into your prayers and try to keep you from the throne of grace. Satan will make every effort to discourage you, to lead you astray, and to guide you away from your prayer path to God. Satan will use discouragement to shake your confidence and shatter your courage. He wants you to give up.

Cindy Jacobs in her book: <u>Possessing the Gates of the Enemy,</u> [21] says, "It takes courage and perseverance to be the kind of intercessor who will make a difference." Don't let Satan discourage you and cause you to wimp through your prayer time. Stand tall, be brave, and build your confidence by never letting up, by "praying without ceasing".

Without question our enemy is Satan and there is no defeat for Satan except through the power of prayer. We do not have the strength to overcome so powerful an enemy without God. But God does not want us to be weak-kneed and namby-pamby in our prayers. God wants real prayer warriors. God wants prayer warriors that will go to battle for His people, whatever the cost.

🏛 Lookout, Satan is hovering. Let's write a prayer of defeat for Satan and victory for us as we continue forward. _____

_____

Hosea 7:6

"For they have made ready their

heart like an oven,

whiles they lie in wait:

their baker sleepeth all the night;

in the morning it burneth as a flaming fire.."

This little verse in Hosea dealt with the Lords indictment of Israel when Israel was in a state of moral depravity. The favor of the Lord had withdrawn His favor and Hosea's marriage to Gomer, the adulterous wife, was symbolic of Israel the adulterous nation. Hosea loved Gomer just as the Lord still loved Israel. Throughout all the heartache and turmoil Hosea kept his passion for the people, always sensitive to their needs. When I came across the verse my imagination ran away with me and I imagined the following picture:

We prepare our hearts like an oven,

While we wait on the call of God,

Asleep in the night,

Until the morning when our passion

Burns like a glowing ember

Our hearts bursting

Ready to meet God.

How wonderful it would be if we woke every morning with a burning passion, boldly going before God with our prayers, or at the night we jump up with excitement and enthusiasm, awakened by God calling on us to pray.

Luke 18: 1 "And he spake a parable unto them to this end, that men ought always to pray, and not to faint;"

Prayer is not for the feint of heart. Prayer is for the brave and strong. When we begin to pray, and throughout our prayers, we must continually turn our thoughts toward God, resisting Satan's interference and binding Satan so he is unable to put a roadblock between us and God. It should not surprise us if in the middle of our prayer time Satan rears his ugly head with the intent to thwart our communion with God. Even as I write this Satan is trying to take over my thoughts. Satan would like nothing better than to see Christians abandon their prayer time and give that time to secular causes. We must remain vigilant in our prayer time, leaning heavily on God, being careful that we do not trust in our own abilities.

Dutch Sheets in his book, <u>Authority in Prayer: Praying with Power and Purpose,</u> says: "We can pray with authority, binding or tying Satan legally, and God will back us with His power."[22] This authority brings confidence and with it the knowledge that God is binding Satan so we can have an effective and powerful prayer life. We must never lose sight of the fact that God is, and has always been, more powerful than Satan.

1 Peter 5:8: "Be sober, be vigilant; because your adversary the devil, as a roaring lion, walketh about, seeking whom he may devour:"

This verse is our warning, our wake up call that reminds us that we must be ever alert to the wiles and ways of Satan. We must be willing to allow God to work in and through us to bind Satan, we must be vigilant.

Life is full of choices and the most important choice we made was to accept Christ as our Savior. Now that we have become Christians we have the privilege and honor of petitioning God for our needs and the needs of others. With that privilege and honor comes another choice, the choice to allow God to reign supreme in our life. We can choose to allow God to bind Satan or we can choose to allow Satan to devour us. Picture a lion with his mouth wide open and your head in his mouth. A frightening picture, yet that is but a small representation of the pain and fear that will lurk in your heart if you let Satan get the upper hand. Where fear reigns, confidence folds.

II Corinthians 10:4-5: [4]***(For the weapons of our warfare are not carnal, but mighty through God to the pulling down of strong holds;)*** [5]***Casting down imaginations, and every high thing that exalteth itself against the knowledge of God, and bringing into captivity every thought to the obedience of Christ;"***

In warfare our confidence wanes if we do not have the proper weapons. If rifles jam, tanks don't run, ammunition is low, body armor is defective and the Commander is hiding, the only confidence we can muster is confidence the enemy will prevail.

II Corinthians 10:4-5 above reminds us that we cannot fight Satan or the evils of this world with defective carnal weapons: weapons of self-righteousness, self-power, self-anything. We can only win when we choose to fight our battles with Christ at our side. When we allow God to intervene on our behalf He will shore up our confidence and our prayer life will take on a new meaning. Let God throw a knock-out punch that flattens Satan and clears a path straight to the throne of grace.

🏛 Write a prayer asking God to give you the confidence and power to pray without fear. Ask God to throw Satan a knock-out punch. _____

_____

_____

_____

Closing Moments

1. Our approach to prayer should be one of _____ and our attitude one

   of _____.

2. Confidence is defined as: _____

   _____

3. Passion, from the Latin word *pati,* means to _____

   _____

4. I Thessalonians 5:17 says _____ _____ _____.

5. Faith defined says we _____and _____ in God and

   are _____to God.

6. Cindy Jacobs, in her book <u>Possessing the Gates of Hell</u>, says: "It takes _____

   __and _____to be a _____that makes a difference.

7. Luke 18:1 says: _____

   _____

SECTION VIII:

DOES FASTING HAVE A PLACE?

Matthew 6:16-18 [16]Moreover when ye fast, be not, as the hypocrites, of a sad countenance: for they disfigure their faces, that they may appear unto men to fast. Verily I say unto you, They have their reward. [17]But thou, when thou fastest, anoint thine head, and wash thy face; [18]That thou appear not unto men to fast, but unto thy Father which is in secret: and thy Father, which seeth in secret, shall reward thee openly."

There are several books on the subject of fasting, but I do not find fasting is as well addressed as other subjects. There are times when it appears fasting is a taboo topic, a topic that if addressed might require a higher commitment in our prayer life. I would like to travel up that road of higher commitment. Why not come along and enjoy the journey with me? Then again it could be a battle, a battle of the carnal and spiritual evils that beset us when we set out to approach God at the throne of His grace. I hope you'll take the challenge.

Fasting touches the core of our carnality. Eating is a carnal, though a necessary evil in our life. Naturally some of us enjoy eating more than others but it is a daily activity that our bodies and minds have gotten used to. Hunger pains begin at birth; they are powerful and drive us straight to the refrigerator or pantry. No wonder fasting is only occasionally addressed as another manner of commitment to prayer.

🏛 Can you remember the last time you fasted and prayed? What were the results? _____

_____

_____

_____

Our dictionary definition deals with fasting only in the area of food. <u>FAST:</u> **1:**to abstain from food **2:** to eat sparingly or abstain from some foods[23]

My view is that fasting can be both abstaining from food and abstaining from other activities in our life. Metaphorically we can abstain from all manner of lusts or anything that is harmful to our prayer life or overall Christian life. We can abstain from food, or just a particular food. This is the most widely accepted definition of fasting. We can also look deeper and not only abstain from food but abstain from any activity that takes us away from our commitment to prayer.

We all have particular activities we enjoy taking part in, such as television, sports events, reading, traveling, and the list goes on. The point is that in and of themselves these activities are not necessarily sinful. They are by nature carnal because they are not of God. God wants us to be happy and enjoy life, but He does not want us to do it at His expense by placing outside activities above Godly pursuits. When we follow worldly pleasures to and exclude our time with God we are enjoying life at God's expense.

What is that one thing, or maybe more than one thing, that means a great deal to your mind and body that you would be willing to give up for God? Can you give up on just one thing for one minute, one hour, one day, or longer? God will reveal what give up and how long we should give it up that if we ask and are willing to listen. Therein lays the challenge of fasting.

Our principal focus will on abstaining from food as that is the most often mentioned type of fasting in the Bible, although other types of abstaining are mentioned.

🏛 What food or activity are you willing to surrender for a time of fasting and prayer? __

_____

I only found one instance in the Bible where there was a command to fast. In Leviticus 23 the Bible talks about the various Feasts, such as the Feast of the First Fruits and the Feast of the Trumpets, as well as the Day of Atonement. If you read this chapter carefully you will find the people were asked at various times to abstain from either all food, a particular food or to abstain from a particular area of work.

The Colombia Encyclopedia describes fasting "as a partial or temporary abstinence from food. Among the stricter Jews the principal fast is the Day of Atonement, or YOM KIPPUR; in Islam the faithful fast all the daytime hours of the month of RAMADAN. Fasting is general in Christianity, the most widely observed fasts are Lent and Advent. Protestants have generally abandoned fasting."[24]

In Matthew 6:17 God refers to fasting as not "if" but "when" you fast. *[17]Moreover when ye fast, be not, as the hypocrites, of a sad countenance:…."*

God expects our fasting to be for God, not to show others how spiritual we are. God does not want us to use fasting as an act of self-glorification. People may notice you are not eating simply because in nowadays you are almost always dining with someone. You may in a position where you need to decline an offer to eat and find the individual asks why you do not wish to eat. This has happened to me. Quietly mention you are fasting and move on to some other conversation. Do not linger on the details. Bragging will cancel any positive effects your fasting might have accomplished.

Matthew 6:17-18 is between the model prayer, referred to most often as the Lord's Prayer, and the verses on laying up your treasures in heaven. If we find the model (Lord's) prayer relevant, and if we believe we should lay up our treasures in heaven, then it only stands to reason that verses 17-18 are just as relevant and just as important. So even without a "thou shalt" commandment to fast, the scriptures do point out that we should, at sometime in our prayer life, fast. Our attitude should be: "not if we fast, but when we fast".

Stop now and write a prayer to God asking for His help in giving you and attitude of "not if, but when" you should fast?_____

_____

_____

There are many instances in the Bible where godly people fasted. Whether for the purpose of removing a particular sin from their life, for healing, restoring a nation, or to propel their mind to higher and more heavenly things, fasting was an important part of their prayer experience. Fasting can be an extremely humbling experience and an important part of your prayer life as well. Always remember that fasting should be a God called and God directed part of your prayer life.

In Daniel 9:1-2 Daniel understood the seventy years of captivity for the Jewish people would soon be over. This prompted Daniel to pray for the people.

Daniel 9:3 says: "And I set my face unto the Lord God, to seek by prayer and supplications, with fasting, and sackcloth, and ashes:"

Daniel's prayer was a prayer of humility. He pointed to his and the peoples sins in contrast to God's righteousness. He sacrificially offered to God every ounce of his being. Daniel reached inside himself to the depths of his heart and soul, and then reached out to God, it is no wonder that he heard from God. Not only did Daniel hear from God, he had a deep faith in God to handle whatever might arise and then trusted God's answer. Daniel fasted for three weeks before he received the vision from the angel. God then gave Daniel a preview of the future of the Jews. I cannot imagine going on a three week fast, nor am I suggesting that anyone should, but that is what God asked Daniel to do and He gave him the strength he needed to do this. Most of us are able to complete a one-day fast (unless there are health issues preventing this) without any problem. What price are we willing to pay? Whatever the price, if God calls you to it, God will guide you through it!

What about when we fast and pray and wrestle with God and God does not respond to our prayer with the answer we requested? We must be willing to accept God's response to our request. God does not always allow us to discern His reasons behind His answers, and God's answers do not always follow our guidelines. However they always follow God's guidelines. Unfortunately, the most common disappointment in prayer is the prayer for healing. We sink our whole being into praying that our loved ones will be healed only to have them pass away. Then we ask why.

David is a classic example of a man who dug deep within himself and fasted with every ounce of his strength and received an answer different for his request. He was a man who gave up food, a comfortable bed and a night with his wife (or wives). David abstained not only from food, but from any carnal desire he might have had. I am sure David did not like the answer he received, but let's read how David handled a difficult situation and a difficult answer to prayer.

II Samuel 12:15-16;19-20 "(15) And Nathan departed unto his house. And the LORD struck the child that Uriah's wife bare unto David, and it was very sick. (16)David therefore besought God for the child; and David fasted, and went in, and lay all night upon the earth…...[19]But when David saw that his servants whispered, David perceived that the child was dead: therefore David said unto his servants, Is the child dead? And they said, He is dead. [20]Then David arose from the earth, and washed, and anointed himself, and changed his apparel, and came into the house of the LORD, and worshipped: then he came to his own house; and when he required, they set bread before him, and he did eat."

We need to stop and think about how we would handle a situation similar to David's? Many of you have been there, so you already know. You have lost a child, a spouse, a parent, a dear friend, or some other precious family member. I realize people handle grief differently and they go through the different stages of grief at different rates of speed. We process the current events in our lives in direct correlation to the past events in our life. How we were taught, or not taught, to handle major life changing events when we were growing up is the foundation for how we handle them now. Those who grew up trusting God, and those who found God later in life, handle their relationship with God differently also.

How do you think all this related to David and how he handled this tragic event in his life? I would contend that as a child David was trained in the proper way to approach and worship God. Not all of us were taught from childhood. Those of us who accepted Christ as adults I hope were taught to worship (as a child of God) from the moment of our spiritual birth. I daresay most of us were not taught that fasting can be an effective part of our prayer life.

How did David handle the death of his son in the verses above? I see a man of God who committed a grievous sin, recognized that sin, but loved the product of the sin, his son. The event leading to the birth of David's son was the sin. There was no sin in loving the child. There was no sin in pleading with God for the child's health. There was no sin in David's attitude of prayer and fasting. Unfortunately where most of us separate ourselves from David is at the end. When all the prayer and fasting are over how do we react to God's divine wisdom, to God's divine answer? Some of us celebrate and some of us become angry, even to the point of bitterness, discouragement and discontentment with God.

David responded by stopping his fasting, cleaning himself up and going to the Lord's house to worship. He worshipped God immediately on receiving the answer to his prayer. God effectively told David he would not be allowed to raise the illegitimate son he bore. Yet David went into the house of God to worship. He dried his tears, worshipped God, and then he ate. Read what David told his servants.

II Samuel 12:22-23 "(22)And he said, While the child was yet alive, I fasted and wept: for I said, Who can tell whether GOD will be gracious to me, that the child may live? (23)But now he is dead, wherefore should I fast? can I bring him back again? I shall go to him, but he shall not return to me."

🏛 Be honest with yourself and think about the last major event in you life where your prayer was not answered in the manner in which you prayed. How did you handle it? Did you move on or are you still back there at the "unanswered" prayer? Write your thoughts here._____

_____

_____

_____

_____

When we decide that fasting is to become an important part of our prayer life we must accept that fasting may not bring the answers we want. Our desired results may not always coincide with God's desired results. We must accept that. I stress this only because I know that when you put every ounce of your being into a particular prayer, it can be a giant spiritual let down when the answer is not what you prayed for. The opposite to that is when you do get the answer you want it is a giant spiritual high. Keep in mind you probably will be the recipient of both the high and the low. It is important to remember that when you receive God's answer to pick yourself up, clean yourself off, worship God, and get something to eat, ready to start over with a new petition for God. Remember, it is not if, but when, God leads you towards fasting and prayer. If you will allow Him, God will use you again and again throughout your Christian life. Prayer and fasting equate to fellowship with God and the more we do it the closer we grow to God.

There are many others in the Bible who fasted and prayed. Let's take a peek at just a few of these great men and women of God.

Nehemiah fasted and prayed over the Jewish survivors from captivity and the wall of Jerusalem being broken and the gates set afire.

Nehemiah 1:4 "And it came to pass, when I heard these words, that I sat down and wept, and mourned certain days, and fasted, and prayed before the God of heaven,"

Esther fasted and prayed when Mordecai told her that Haman had gone to the King and received permission to do with the Jews as he saw fit. Haman (Esther 3:13) had the King sign a decree ordering the annihilation of all the Jews. Mordecai asked Esther to go to the King, an act which was forbidden if the King had not called the person to his inner court.

Esther 4:16 "Go, gather together all the Jews that are present in Shushan, and fast ye for me, and neither eat nor drink three days, night or day: I also and my maidens will fast likewise; and so will I go in unto the king, which is not according to the law: and if I perish, I perish."

Anna fasted and prayed as a way of life.

Luke 2:37 "And she was a widow of about fourscore and four years, which departed not from the temple, but served God with fastings and prayers night and day."

Cornelius was told to send for Simon Peter who was of the gentile nation because of his fasting and praying. This was an unlawful act for a Jewish person.

Acts 10:30-31 "(30)And Cornelius said, Four days ago I was fasting until this hour; and at the ninth hour I prayed in my house, and, behold, a man stood before me in bright clothing, (31)And said, Cornelius, thy prayer is heard, and thine alms are had in remembrance in the sight of God."

Christians fasted and prayed and received instructions from the Lord in furthering the work of those called of God to be missionaries.

Acts 13:1-3: "(1) Now there were in the church that was at Antioch certain prophets and teachers; as Barnabas, and Simeon that was called Niger, and Lucius of Cyrene, and Manaen, which had been brought up with Herod the tetrarch, and Saul. (2)As they ministered to the Lord, and fasted, the Holy Ghost said, Separate me Barnabas and Saul for the work whereunto I have called them. 3)And when they had fasted and prayed, and laid their hands on them, they sent them away."

Compared to those men and women of God our efforts pale by comparison, however, it is not our place to compare ourselves to others so much as it is to follow their example. What type of fasting, or how long a fast, God leads us to may not be as extreme but it will be within our abilities to fulfill the task if we are willing.

Fasting is just one more tool in your fight to defeat the powers of Satan. When we fast we are serving Satan with notice that we are in control of our bodies, our body does not control us. We claim Christ as our power and strength, He is our sustainer, and Satan is the defeated.

This study is almost completed; we only have one chapter to go. Has God placed on you heart a special person or event, a special something to pray about? What has God laid on your heart?_____

_____

_____

Closing Moments

1. How does the dictionary define fasting?_____

   _____

2. Is food the only means of fasting? _____ Explain your answer. _____

   _____

3. Where in the Bible do we find a command to fast?_____

4. Matthew 6:17-18 refers to fasting as not _____ but _____ we fast.

5. Fasting and prayer do not always bring the results we want. What was David's reaction

   when his son died? See II Sam 12:22-23. _____

   _____

   _____

6. Go back and name others who fasted and prayed. What were the results? _____

   _____

   _____

   _____

SECTION IX:

THE BEGINNING

Philippians 4:8 "Finally, brethren, whatsoever things are true, whatsoever things are honest, whatsoever things are just, whatsoever things are pure, whatsoever things are lovely, whatsoever things are of good report; if there be any virtue, and if there be any praise, think on these things."

We are coming to the end of our journey and we have covered much ground in just a few short chapters. The intent of this study guide was not to make it so long and drawn out that you became bogged down in a mire of excess words. The purpose was to consolidate a multitude of information in a format that was easy to follow and easy to put into practice. I trust I have succeeded in doing just that.

We have prayed throughout this study but now the real test begins. Are we willing to begin a lifetime of commitment to prayer and fasting, a prayer life far above and beyond anything we have done before? Now we must allow God to mold us and make us into an intercessory prayer warrior. We can sit through lesson after lesson and walk out no more committed than when we came in if we fail to allow God to encompass our heart. We must be willing to follow His guidance and direction as we embark on a life of intercessory prayer.

I was listening to a speaker on the radio who told about how she had difficulty finding time to pray. That sounded all too familiar. The speaker relayed how she always found time to carry out the daily routines of her life, but her prayer life was sporadic. She realized she was failing to set aside a time for prayer. She scheduled time for her everyday routines and miscellaneous activities and appointments, but not time with God. She committed to make an appointment with God to talk to him for one hour a day and has done so for the past 20 years. Have you found that it has been difficult to make time for this study? Has it been difficult to make time for prayer? Why not make an appointment with God? We make appointments for everything else and we keep those appointments, why not with God?

When God led me to the person who was to become my prayer partner we scheduled a morning every week and a specific time to meet. There were times when we could not meet but when we were not able to meet I still devoted that period of time to God, as I am sure my prayer partner did as well. Let's make an appointment with God today. It is always easy to say that you will get to it later, but it seems later never comes. Instead busy comes and we push away God's time. We need to get in the habit of coming to God daily, not only at our prearranged time, but throughout the day as well. God not only enjoys our hour, more or less, of committed time for prayer, but He enjoys the little chats we have with Him off and on all-day long.

🏛 Why not make an appointment now and write the time here? _____

I find that by starting my prayer time with Praise and Worship my heart begins to sense the presence of God. I go off by myself and sing to the Lord and tell Him how great and mighty He is. I have a conversation with God and spill all my secret thoughts, my worries and concerns. Not asking God for anything I confess to whatever's inside me so I will be clean when I do ask for something. I need to bask in the presence of God until I am one with Him, otherwise when I begin to petition God it's like hitting a brick wall. God likes a sweet odor, not a stench because we refuse to clean up our hearts and minds. If we come clean with God, God will clean us up so our petitions will fly to heaven. We need to get rid of those cobwebs of the heart and mind.

As we leave this study group it will be important that you choose someone to be your prayer partner. If you are doing this study on your own you may want to call someone and invite them to be your prayer partner. God promises where two or three are gathered He will be in the midst thereof (Matthew 18:20). With a prayer partner we not only strengthen our prayers but we place ourselves in a position of accountability where we become answerable to another person for our actions. If we have a definite time and place to meet we are not as likely to skip our prayer time, it helps us to stand firm in our commitment. We are less likely to skip over our commitment when someone else is aware of what we have committed to do. I equate this with going forward and announcing that you have accepted Christ as your Savior. When it is out in the open we are more likely to follow through on our commitment.

Your prayer partner can be someone you have prayed with throughout this study or someone outside this group. Pray about whom God would have you become a partner with. When I realized my need to have a prayer partner I initially thought of friends around me, co-workers, people I admired. I even asked a couple of people. Maybe it was more of an invitation to come pray with me once or twice. I admired and respected all these people and sincerely believed they were people of prayer. But, alas, none of them worked out.

🏛 Who is the first person that comes to mind?_____

Just because you admire and respect someone does not necessarily mean that is the person who God wants you partnered with. PRAY! PRAY! PRAY! God will partner you with someone you might not expect, but he or she will be someone you can look up to and respect. I believe God will choose just the right prayer partner for you. When you think you know who that person is it would be prudent to discover if you and your prayer partner are of a like mind.

We are human and have been known to put our wants in the place of God's leading. You can be certain that you are probably in concert with God if you consider the following about the person.

First and foremost be sure that he or she is a Christian. Share your testimony with each other. Give your account of how and when you came to a saving knowledge of the Lord Jesus Christ. It is always encouraging and spiritually uplifting to go back and relive that time when God lifted you up out of the mire of sin. Whether you accepted Christ as a child, or later in life, the Cross of Calvary is no less exciting.

Second discuss your doctrinal stand on biblical matters. For example: Where do you stand on heaven? Where do you stand on everlasting life? What are your beliefs about the rapture of the saints? What do you think about abortion? Do you believe in the doctrine of "once saved always saved"? **John 10:28 says:** *"And I give unto them eternal life; and they shall never perish, neither shall any man pluck them out of my hand."*

Discuss what is important to you and make sure you and your prayer partner are of a like mind. This does not mean you have to agree on everything that comes up, but it does mean that Biblically and doctrinally you are agreed. Do not be legalistic in your beliefs, but do stand up for sound doctrine. I stress doctrine because we have opinions. Our opinions are changeable and it does not matter if you and your prayer partner share the same opinions on everything. The saying "agree to disagree" is a good maxim to follow.

Once you are sure you and your partner have been partnered by God set aside a time, at least once a week, when you will meet and pray together. During this time you will share the burden, or burdens, God has laid on your heart. Keep a notebook and write down these burdens and continue to pray for them daily until you meet again or until you know the prayer has been answered.

Have you been praying? Is the person you named above the one God has placed on your heart? Has God given you a new name?_____

You will probably start out with just one or maybe two burdens. In time you will have more. No burden is too small or too big. All burdens for prayer are given to you by God. Remember this is a special prayer time for special burdens and does not take the place of your regular prayer time with God where you petition Him on a personal level about personal needs, family needs, general church needs, etc. It is not to say God may not use this time occasionally for you to pray on a personal level. You must always be open to God's leading, but generally this time should be set aside for those special burdens God places on your heart.

1 Peter 1:13 "Wherefore gird up the loins of your mind, be sober, and hope to the end for the grace that is to be brought unto you at the revelation of Jesus Christ."

An important step in this process is to prepare ourselves for prayer. This might sound strange but before we go to pray with our prayer partner, we must pray. There are cleansing and healing prayers that we need to carry out before we meet with our prayer partner.

In Psalm 139:23-24 it says "²³⁾Search me, O God, and know my heart: try me, and know my thoughts: ²⁴⁾And see if there be any wicked way in me, and lead me in the way everlasting."

We must allow God to try us and search our hearts, confess before God any sins we may have entertained or may be entertaining and approach God with a clean heart.

Generally you will both pray aloud and petition God on an individual personal level as well as a partnership level. However, be open to the possibility that God may only want one person to pray and the other to quietly petition the Holy Spirit. Do not think that you are obligated to burst out in vocal prayer just because you are meeting. Sometimes your heart is just too heavy and hurts too much to pray aloud. That's when it is time to let your partner share the load.

Psalm 35: 13 "But as for me, when they were sick, my clothing was sackcloth: I humbled my soul with fasting; and my prayer returned into mine own bosom."

Remember, prayer can be a burden, a God placed burden. It is an honor and a privilege to carry that burden to God. As we come to the end of this study I want you to picture in your mind that you are standing before Jesus. Can you sense His presence and His warmth, His Love and His Mercy? Now picture kneeling before Him and placing all your burdens, and the burdens you carry for others, at His feet. Now imagine Jesus reaching down and picking up each burden gently and carefully, examining each need, each petition, looking down with such tenderness saying "yes my child, your desire is my desire". Maybe He will say; "no child, I cannot give that but what I offer will be so much better. I Love you so much I just want to give you what you need". Then Jesus touches you with those nail pierced hands and you experience His love like you've never experienced it before. It is a love so foreign to the world that it can only be the love of God offered through the sacrifice of His Son at Calvary. Can you sense the warmth of his shed blood as you humbly bow before Him?

That image can be yours if you keep God at the top of your list of priorities. Place Him above all else and your prayer life will be one of friendship, companionship, and continuing fellowship with God the Father, God the Son and God the Holy Spirit.

Romans 12:2 "And be not conformed to this world: but be ye transformed by the renewing of your mind, that ye may prove what is that good, and acceptable, and perfect, will of God.."

Amen

Closing Moments

1. The radio speaker suggested we make an _____ with God to _____.

2. We need to get rid of those _____ of the heart and mind.

3. What should you consider first when selecting a prayer partner? _____

4. What else should you look at? _____

   _____

5. What scripture was used to stress preparing yourself for prayer? _____

   Write the scripture here. _____

   _____

   _____

6. Remember, Prayer is a God placed burden. Write out Psalm 35:13 _____

   _____

   _____

1 Dutch Sheets, *The Beginners Guide to Intercession* (p.13., © by Servant Publications now Gospel Light/Regal Books, Ventura Ca 93003. 2001,13. Used by permission)

2 James Strong, STD, LLD, Strong's Concordance, (Abingdon, Nashville, 1976, Main Concordance,804-805)

3 Matthew Henry Concise, (Epiphany Software, 1995)

4 Pfeiffer, Vos, Rea: *Wycliff Bible Encyclopedia*, (Moody Bible Institute of Chicago, 1979, Vol I, 850)

5 The Living Webster Encyclopedic Dictionary of the English Language, (The English Language Institute of America, Inc, 1974, 501)

6 Norman Grubb: *Rees Howells Intercessor*: (The Lutterworth Press, Cambridge, CB1 2NT, England 1952,) (94-97)

7 Ibid: (115)

8 Ibid: (94-97)

9 This text was converted to ascii format for Project Wittenberg by Rev. Robert E. Smith of the Walther Library at Concordia Theological Seminary and is in the public domain. You may freely distribute, copy or print this text.

10 Charles Haddon Spurgeon, *Spurgeon's Sermons, Vol. 4 (Grand Rapids: Baker Book House, 1983), 351*

11 The Living Webster Encyclopedic Dictionary of the English Language, (*English LanguageInstitute,1974,695*)

12 Ibid; (707)

13 The Living Webster Encyclopedic Dictionary of the English Language, (*English LanguageInstitute,1974,695*)

14 Jim Cymballa, *Breakthrough Prayer,* (Zondervan, 2003) (88)

15 James Strong, STD, LLD, Strong's Concordance, (Abingdon, Nashwille, 1976,Hebrew and Chaldee Dictionary,97)

16 "By permission. From the *Merriam-Webster Online Dictionary* ©2007 by Merriam-Webster Inc. (ww.Merriam-Webster.com)."

17 Ibid

18 Ibid

19 Ibid

20 Ibid

21 Jacobs, Cindy, *Possessing the Gates of the Enemy,*(Chosen Books, a division of Baker Publishing Group, 1991,1994) (23)

22 Sheets, Dutch, *Authority in Prayer: Praying with Power and Purpose, (Bethany House Publishers, 2006) (22)*

23 "By permission. From the *Merriam-Webster Online Dictionary* ©2007 by Merriam-Webster Inc. (ww.Merriam-Webster.com)

24 Lagass, 🏛. P., & Columbia University. (2000). *The Columbia encyclopedia* (6th ed.). New York; Detroit: Columbia University Press; Sold and distributed by Gale Group. 1 The Columbia Encyclopedia, Sixth Edition. Copyright © 2001-05 Columbia University Press. NEW YORK: COLUMBIA UNIVERSITY PRESS, 2001–05 NEW YORK: BARTLEBY. COM, 2001–05 UPDATED: JULY, 2005

BIBLIOGRAPHY:

1. Dutch Sheets: The Beginners Guide to Intercession ©*2001, Vine Books, an imprint of Servant Publications*

2. Dutch Sheets: Intercessory Prayer ©*1996 Regal Books from Gospel Light*

3. Dutch Sheets: Authority in Prayer ©*2006 Bethany House Publishers*

4. Dutch Sheets: Study Guide ©*2004 Regal Books from Gospel Light*

5. Norman Grubb: Rees Howells, Intercessor ©*1952,2002 Lutterworth Press*

6. Mina Kohlhafer: Workbook for Rees Howell, Intercessor *1993 Christian Literature Crusade*

7. E.M. Bounds: Purpose in Prayer ©*1997, Whitaker House*

8. E.M. Bounds: Prayer and Spiritual Warfare ©*1984 Whitaker House*

9. Derek Prince: Fasting ©*1986, Whitaker House*

10. Ed Dufresne: Praying Gods Word ©*1982 Whitaker House*

11. Jim Cymbala: Breakthrough Prayer ©*2003 Zondervan*

12. Cindy Jacobs: Possessing the Gates of the Enemy ©*1991, 1994, 2005 Chosen Books, A division of Baker Publishing Group*

13. Andrew Murray: Teach Me to Pray ©*1982, 2002, Bethany House Publishers*

14. Terry Teykl: Intercessor's Handbook ©*1999 Prayer Point Press*

15. Jim George: The Remarkable Prayers of the Bible ©*2005, Harvest House Publishers*

11. Bruce Wilkinson: The Prayer of Jabez ©*2002 Multnomah Publishers, Inc*

16. L. Richards: Every Prayer in the Bible ©*1998, T. Nelson; Nashville*

17. J.V. McGee: Thru the Bible commentary (electronic edition) ©*1997, c1981, Thomas Nelson, Nashville*

18. Pray Magazine: ©*Navpress (800) 691-7729*

19. W. Vine: Vine's complete expository dictionary and topic finder. ©*1997, 1996 (electronic ed) Thomas Nelson, Nashville*

20. J. Strong: Enhanced Strong's Lexicon ©*1996 Woodside Bible Fellowship, Ontario*

21. J.W. Hayford & J. Snider: Kingdom Power, a study in the book of Acts ©*1993, 1997 Thomas Nelson, Nashville*

22. J.W. Hayford & Thomas Nelson Publishers: Hayford's Bible Handbook ©*1995Thomas Nelson Publishers*

23. Matthew Henry Concise ©*1995 Epihany Software*

25. Youngblood, R.R., Bruce, F.F., Harrison, R.K. & Thomas Nelson Publishers: Gentiles ©*1995 Nelsons new illustrated Bible dictionary. T Nelson, Nashville*

26. J. Swanson & O. Nave: New Naves: Intercession & Prayerfulness ©*1994 Logos Research Systems: Oak Harbor*

27. L. Richards: Every prayer in the Bible ©*1998 Thomas Nelson, Nashville*

28. Libronix Digital Library System 3.0c © *2002-2006 Libronix Corporation*

29. Various Web Sites that were very helpful:

http://www.aboutbibleprophecy.com/abraham.htm

http://www.biblegateway.com/versions /

http://www.ccel.org/

http://www.prayerleader.com/index.ph

http://www.armed-prayer.org/

http://www.universalteacher.org.uk/bible/biblepeople.htm

http://www.christiananswers.net/dictionary/

http://www.navpress.com/Magazines/Pray!/

Printed in the United States
97427LV00002B/229-1000/A

9 781604 773156